RACHEL SUMMERS

WILD ADVENT

DISCOVERING GOD THROUGH CREATION

kevin mayhew

kevin
mayhew

First published in Great Britain in 2018 by Kevin Mayhew Ltd
Buxhall, Stowmarket, Suffolk IP14 3BW
Tel: +44 (0) 1449 737978 Fax: +44 (0) 1449 737834
E-mail: info@kevinmayhew.com

www.kevinmayhew.com

9 8 7 6 5 4 3 2 1 0

ISBN 978 1 84867 960 3
Catalogue No. 1501583

Cover design by Rob Mortonson
© Images used under licence from Shutterstock Inc.
Typeset by Angela Selfe
Printed and bound in Great Britain

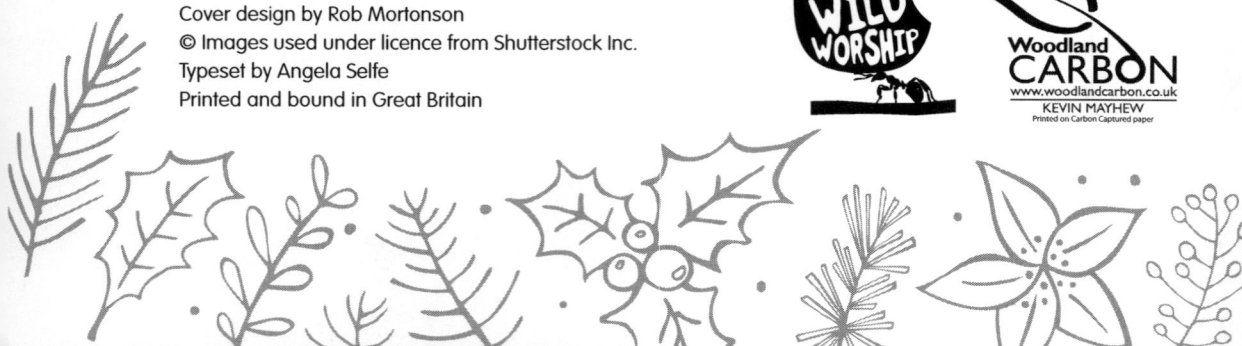

WILD WORSHIP

Woodland CARBON
www.woodlandcarbon.co.uk
KEVIN MAYHEW
Printed on Carbon Captured paper

CONTENTS

Short and easy things to make and do

Even shorter things to do

ABOUT THE AUTHOR

Rachel lives in a vicarage in East London with her husband, their five kids, and a veritable menagerie of pets. She loves her corner of the urban wild, and the fact that within a few minutes she can be surrounded by the multicultural busyness of the market, awed by the wide expanse of the marshes, or enclosed amongst the ancient trees of Epping Forest.

A teacher by trade, and daughter of the highly successful author, Susan Sayers, Rachel moved from teaching in primary schools, through doing work one-to-one with excluded teens, to retraining as a forest school practitioner. She now delivers forest school sessions to nurseries, schools, and the general public. Although she never quite manages to scrub the mud off her hands, Rachel believes she has the best job in the world.

Sharing the magic of all things slimy and interesting, watching the seasons shift and the weather change, finding the beauty in the commonplace and insignificant, holding space for others to explore: these are some of the things which get Rachel excited. She gives thanks for the people, communities and world that God has given her to live in and be a part of, and takes delight in sharing that joy with others.

@wildworshipuk   wildworshipuk

WHY WILD ADVENT?

There are definitely benefits to spending time outside, especially as the days grow darker. Throughout Advent you are very aware of the darkness growing, as you draw near the winter solstice on 21 December. It's easy to go into hibernation mode, and you really have to challenge yourself to get out and engage with the world outside. But it's worth it.

Two scientific studies from 2013 point to the benefits of nature on our stress levels – one found that viewing images from nature helped participants to cope with a stressful task better, and the other found that listening to sounds from nature helped participants recover from a stressful situation more readily. The practice of what is called 'forest bathing' has become widespread in Japan since the 1980s, where people visit the forest for relaxation and stress management.

Not all of us are lucky enough to live with a forest on our doorstep, or a beautiful natural environment a short walk away. If you do, then by all means enjoy it and take full advantage of it! However, even the most urban of environments can give us a chance to connect with the natural world. Everyone has access to the sky, which is always changing. Sometimes it's clear and high. Sometimes it is painted with a spectacular sunset. Sometimes it's dark and brooding and about to burst. Most areas have a few trees, and there are weeds and grass that grow between cracks on the pavement and by the sides of railway bridges. Some of this may not be splendid, but if you take the time to look it can still be awe-inspiring.

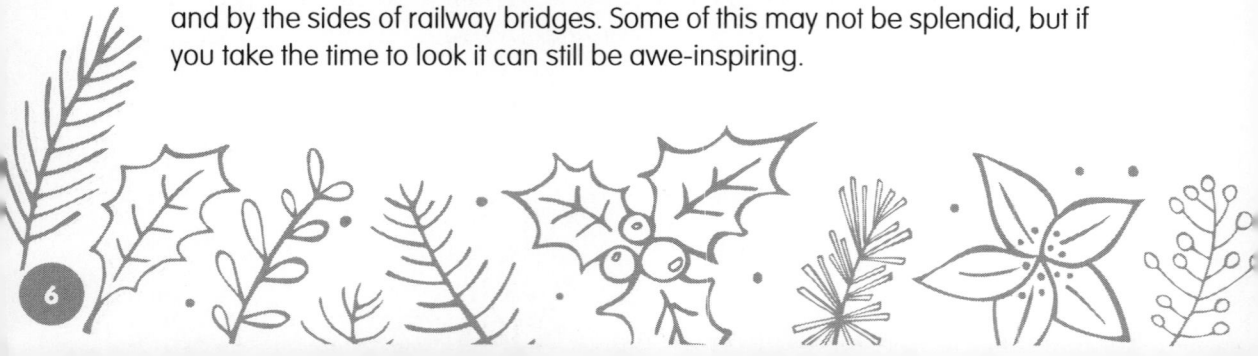

With the best will in the world, the run-up to Christmas can be an exhausting and frenetic business. We are sucked more and more into preparations at home, parties at work or at school, services in church buildings, and walking endless corridors in an air-conditioned shopping centre. Some of this is exciting, and most of this is all good preparation, and nearly all of it is necessary. However, stepping outside all of this can give us much-needed time to reflect on what Advent means, to think about what we're really waiting for, to give us some calm in the middle of the chaos. And I'm talking here about literally stepping outside. We can bring Advent with us, by all means, but the natural world will inspire us in a way we are unable to find indoors.

After all, creation is one of the ways in which God speaks to us. Many people find they feel closest to God when they are outdoors. John Muir, a famous nature lover, wrote, 'And into the forest I go, to lose my mind and find my soul.' The Bible, too, acknowledges how nature can speak to us of God. In Psalm 19:1 (NIV) we hear that, 'The heavens declare the glory of God; the skies proclaim the work of his hands', and in his letter to the Romans, Paul tells us that, 'Ever since the creation of the world his eternal power and divine nature, invisible though they are, have been understood and seen through the things he has made' (1:20, NRSV). So much of the worship of the church is tied up with doing things in a building; maybe it's time for us to step outside and listen.

Through the ideas in this book, and trying to keep a 'Wild Advent', you will be able to spend time outside all the busyness, finding that still, small voice where God can speak to you through the world that he has made. This world is a gift; unwrapping a small parcel of it every day is surely the most joy-filled way we can spend our Advent.

HOW THIS BOOK WORKS

This book provides you with a pick and mix of activities you can do that will give you a chance to connect with the natural world around you, and listen to what God is saying to you through it. There are enough activities to do one a day throughout the four weeks of Advent, and these are set out over four themes, giving you a sense of movement and progression across the season: **waiting, accepting, journeying, birthing**. These traditional Carmelite themes for Advent will scaffold our Wild Advent experience.

Each activity includes reflections on two different themes, enabling you to revisit one activity twice over the season if you so wish. Don't feel you have to limit yourself to my reflections – they are just there to act as a guide as you begin to feel yourself into reflecting on creation as the fifth gospel, part of the good news of God and salvation, and listening to the wisdom to be found there. The more you practise this, the more natural you'll find it.

The same goes also for the short prayers at the end of the reflections. If you've received something different from the activity than I have done, then your prayer will obviously reflect this instead. And that's more than fine, of course!

As the activities are rooted and grounded in your experience of being outdoors, you'll end up spending this Advent keeping watch on the sky, and on your weather app on your phone. Some activities can be done in any weather, but it's worth seizing the chance of any cold snap or clear night, and changing your plans appropriately.

There are spaces for you to journal and keep notes about your own experiences through your Wild Advent. Hopefully this will become something special to look back on. If you post your experiences on social media using the hashtag #wildadvent, you will be able to inspire and be inspired by others following the same journey online.

THINGS TO DO WHEN IT'S COLD

Things to do when it's cold...

find some frost

See page 22

experience hail, sleet or freezing rain

See page 18

make snow taffy

See page 26

←tray of snow

create icy decorations

See page 16

breathe
like a baby
dragon...

See page 20

See page 14

create your own
icicles

CREATE YOUR OWN ICICLE

We were walking to school one icy morning, when my children noticed that one of the grimy water outlets from a building near the railway bridge had sprouted sparkling icicles overnight. Suddenly, this rather dirty, unkempt, leaky building in need of repair, had turned into something rather special. With the sunlight glinting off the icicles, the waste pipe was made spectacularly beautiful.

We walked the rest of the way working out how we could make our own icicle to enjoy at home. That evening we rigged up a container full of water, balanced diagonally and precariously on the leftover jam jar tealights from another evening, and draped a length of wool over the edge. We watched to check it was dripping, then left it overnight. In the morning – no icicle, just a kind of icy stalagmite lump. A bit disappointing! The next evening we tried poking a few holes in the bottom of an ice-cream tub (if you heat a needle, it slides in nice and easily), filling it with water, and hanging it up, somewhat drippily, from one of our trees in the garden. The next morning, aha! an icicle! A really rather tiny one, but definitely an icicle all the same.

Maybe with a bit of experimentation, you'll do better than us!

Waiting

'It won't happen overnight', we say. We know that change is often incremental. Sitting and waiting and watching for an icicle to form would be an impossible lesson in patience! It would certainly not be something that my children would manage, and to be honest I think it would be outside my capabilities too. In the case of an icicle though, if we get the set-up right, and read the weather app correctly on our phone, then it might well happen overnight. As you wait for the dripping and the cold to work their magic, does this speak to you of anything else in your life, or in your wider community, or the world that you live in? What if, as in my first experience of icicle making, your waiting seems to bear no result?

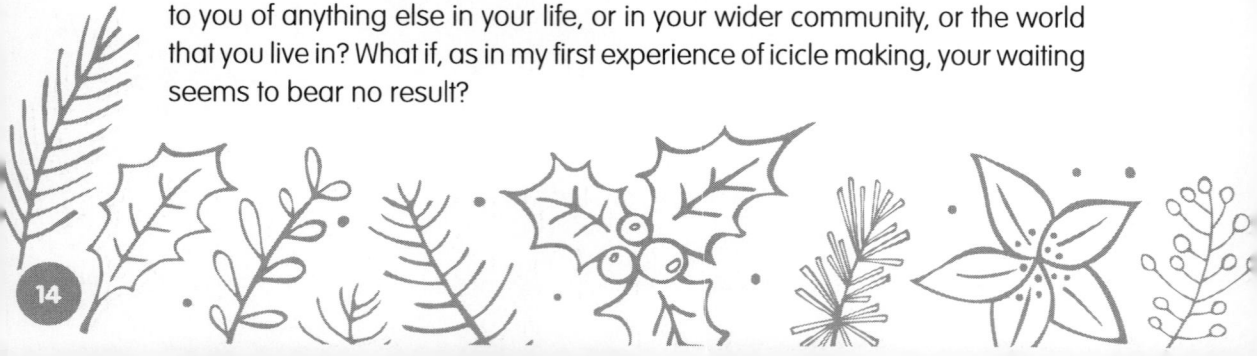

Lord, wait with me as I long for change.
Give me your peace as I struggle with patience.
Amen.

Accepting

It was through my children seeing past the muck and grime of the building on our way to school, that we were able to be filled with wonder at the icicle we saw. When our first icicle attempt went awry, we were disappointed. What we saw didn't match up to our vision. But sometimes it's important to simply see. What we'd made wasn't an icicle, but looking for an icicle where there wasn't one would be a waste of time. Far better to see clearly what we had made, enjoy it for what it was, and not what we wished it might be. Even the garden, frosty and pale in the early morning, was a gift. As you attempt your icicle, you might attempt also to see and enjoy clearly what is, as well as what you wish will be.

Lord, give me your clear vision to see the beauty
in the world as it is, as well as the beauty that
is to come.
Amen.

CREATE ICY DECORATIONS

Sometimes, after a hard frost you go out in your garden and find that all those containers that have ended up lurking in your garden, filling up with rain and blown leaves, are now full of ice. You can tap the ice out, and what was just murky old water now looks rather magical.

How much more, then, if you leave out containers of water on purpose? Collect some small bowls, saucers, and lids, and place them in the coldest corner of your outside space. Take yourself off on a wander around to find interesting natural objects to add to your decorations. You might find bright berries, green leaves from laurel, holly, or fir trees, dusky grey sprigs of lavender, multi-coloured autumn leaves, and nuts and seeds.

Arrange these inside the containers, and pour in water. Add a loop of wool or string, weighing it down so the ends are securely underneath the water, then leave it overnight. When you check in the morning, as long as it's been cold enough, the water will have set firm, freezing the treasures in place. Tap them out of the containers – the loop of wool will mean that you're able to hang these decorations outside, maybe from a tree. Enjoy them sparkling in the morning light for the short time that they last.

Journeying

The change of water into ice is quite interesting. In essentials, it is the same substance – still made up out of molecules comprised of one oxygen and two hydrogen atoms. As the temperature drops, heat is transferred out of the water into the surroundings. As the energy of the heat is removed from the water, the molecules move slower and slower. The bonds between the hydrogen atoms result in the water turning into a crystalline structure: ice. And, unusually, the solid form of water is less dense than it is as a liquid. Anyone who's dealt with the fallout from a burst water pipe after a freeze, or a bottle left too long in the freezer, will also be very aware that ice takes up more space than water. Nine per cent more, in fact. As we think about our journeying this Advent, we remember how, like ice, it is our bonds with

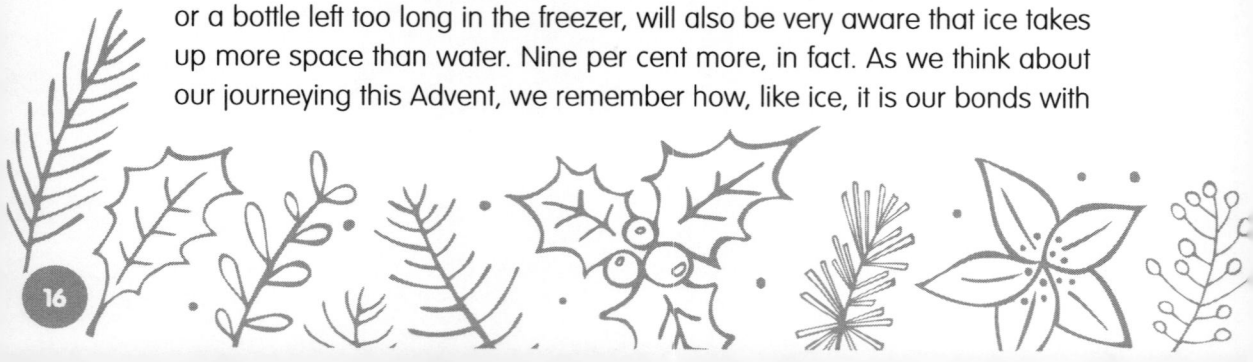

others that draw us together and make us strong in difficult times, and how together we are greater than we could be alone.

> Lord, change due to circumstances outside our control can feel frightening or unpleasant. Help us to grow strong bonds with those around us, so that together we can be bigger and stronger than we would be alone.
> Amen.

Birthing

To create anything, you have to find the right situation and the right environment. You may wish to make ice decorations in the middle of the summer, as maybe there'd be so much more choice of colours and shapes in the summer flowers and leaves, but no matter how beautiful they looked inside the containers filled with water, leaving them outside in your garden wouldn't result in anything more than tiny pretty puddles. You, however, here in the frozen days of winter, will have more luck. Working with your environment rather than against it, using and treasuring what is special about what you actually have, knowing and understanding its limits and its possibilities; that's a pretty good lesson God's creation can give us. Next time we start to dream of plans, of creations, we may remember this, and work within the parameters of the environment surrounding us, using its possibilities as an opening rather than a prison.

> Lord, help me to see the potential in the situations I find myself in, and to use it to create beauty for everyone to enjoy.
> Amen.

FIND FROST

In the summer, when the conditions are right, moisture condensing from the air overnight appears as dew. In the winter, this moisture appears as frost, which looks different depending on the humidity and temperature of the night. Walking across frosted grass is so satisfying, as your foot first meets the resistance of the ice, then crunches through, leaving a trail of footprints behind you.

My kids enjoy scraping patterns and messages into the covering of frost on the wooden benches and bin lids on their way to school on cold mornings. Sometimes they manage to scratch off enough frost to make a teeny tiny, centimetre high frostman. Enjoy the spectacle of frost on your car window before you scrape it off and start the engine, or on a window of a shed or garage. Notice how the ice has grown in a fractal, looking like ferns or feathers. Seek out spiders' webs, and enjoy how the hoar frost turns them from a Halloween decoration into a Christmas one! 'Hoar' comes from the old English, meaning 'showing signs of old age', because of how it makes bushes and trees look like they've sprouted white beards.

Look also for examples of more unusual frosts. Needle ice occurs in areas of land where there is flowing water just under the surface. When the temperature above the land is below zero, but the land is still above freezing point, the water below ground is brought to the surface little by little, freezing into a column. Frost flowers occur when the sap in a plant begins to freeze, and little by little more sap is drawn up and frozen, adding to the petal-like appearance of the ice. You may be lucky enough to find some hair ice, shaped and grown on rotten wood, looking like threads of silky hair. It's a particular fungus that creates the ice this way, adding a form of antifreeze that stabilises the ice formation, stopping it from recrystallising into larger crystals.

Journeying

Stepping out into a frosty world can be a little disorientating. Not only does the cold air tickle your nose, and as you pull on and zip up more layers you find the cold is grabbing you quicker than you'd expected, with the warmth

of your bed, and your home, and your morning cup of tea evaporating faster than you'd like, but also a white frost-covered world looks different from normal. With your world in monochrome, it's harder to differentiate between the grass and the concrete, between rocks and clumps of soil. You are struck by how similar some things look that normally would appear quite different. Maybe the brightness of the sunshine reflected off the frost dazzles your eyes. In Advent, we have the chance to look at old, familiar stories and narratives anew, allowing them to dazzle us with their brightness, and for certain parts of them to stand out and be noticed in a new way.

> Lord, as I travel once again through the narrative of the story of your salvation, allow it to shock me, to dazzle me, and let me notice new things that stand out for me particularly this year.
> Amen.

Birthing

The patterns of frost look random and haphazard at first sight, as they crazy-pave their way across your car windscreen. It's hard to notice the pattern behind the chaos. But looking closer at your patch of frost, you begin to make out the crystalline nature of it – you can see how one crystal has led on to another, mathematically scribbling geometric shapes. A message from the water in the air to you, telling you of the weather conditions in which it was made. The birth of the Messiah begins right back with the creation of pattern out of chaos, and the form that the Messiah takes, a vulnerable newborn human child, speaks of the God from which he came. Looking over those things which are coming to birth in you, what patterns can you notice? How do they speak of the conditions in which they were made, and how might they be changed and shaped by the birth of this Messiah?

> Lord, as I see the patterns through my own chaos, show me how my life may be changed by your birth.
> Amen.

BREATHE LIKE A BABY DRAGON

This is surely something that nobody ever grows out of. I can remember as a child, walking to school on a frosty winter morning, and being thrilled at how I could puff out clouds. If you were to pass me in the street as I dash back from the school run, or run up the high street to my choir on a Wednesday evening, you may well spot me still puffing out clouds as I go. In my head, I'm still a baby dragon. I never did quite graduate to breathing fire, but breathing out clouds of smoke (or water vapour) is still almost a superpower, I reckon.

The air you breathe out is more moist than the air you breathe in, having travelled through your wet lungs and your wet mouth. While it was inside your nice warm damp lungs, the moisture was able to stay as a gas, but when you breathe it out into the cold air, the water in your breath no longer has the energy to stay in a gaseous state, and condenses into water droplets and ice crystals, just as water vapour does up in the clouds. Your breath, being full of water, forms a small cloud of its own before dispersing into the environment.

You can play around with this a bit. Get a few of you together and see if you can create a bigger cloud. How long does your cloud last before you can't see it any more? What about if you bring out a cup of tea, and take a couple of nice hot sips first before breathing out as hard as you can? Does this make for a better cloud? And, of course, you can have lots of fun imagining you are a baby dragon, no matter how old you are!

Waiting

You can't make a cloud just by moving air around. Squeezing a bicycle pump, or the bellows from a fireplace may mimic a breath, but the effect will be precisely nothing. It's what happens inside, in the hidden secrets of your lungs, your throat and your mouth, that will allow the cloud to form. Feel as you take that breath in, and as it fills your lungs. Sense the damp warmth of your body warming up that cold air and it absorbing some of your body's moisture. Feel that cavity of your body filled with the air that was once outside. What are the hidden things in your life, the hidden changes, taking

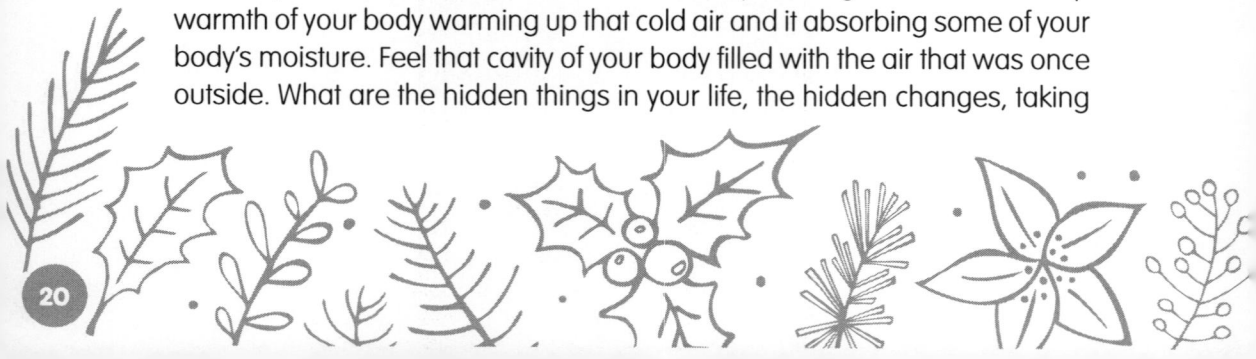

place this Advent? Notice them and value them, remembering that it's not always the spectacular and visible that's important. Don't rush this waiting – sometimes important things take time. In Ezekiel 37:14 (CEB) God speaks: 'I will put my breath in you, and you will live.' You are full of the breath, of the life, of the Spirit of God.

> Lord, as I notice the breath that fills me, help me also be aware that I am filled with your Spirit, and to rest in the spaces between breaths.
> Amen.

Birthing

Humans are innately creative creatures. It's very satisfying to make something appear in a space where there was nothing, even if it's only a small cloud on a cold day. Similar to the reasons for the rise of the selfie, it's comforting to have proof that we exist. There's something special about the interaction between our environment, our bodies, and our mind and will. As you experiment with creating a bigger or better cloud, with friends or with a hot drink, think through what else you are bringing to birth in your life at the moment. What are you creating in a place where there was nothing? Who and what are you working with to make it bigger and better?

> Lord, as I breathe a new cloud into being, lead me and guide me as I breathe new things into being in my life also.
> Amen.

HAIL, SLEET AND FREEZING RAIN

You've probably heard that Eskimos have over a hundred words for snow. This was widely believed to be a bit of a myth until an anthropologist recently discovered that Central Siberian Yupik has 40, while Inuit spoken in Canada's Nunavik region has at least 53. It pays to get specific with the type of weather you encounter a lot. In Britain we have a lot of different names for rain – pouring, drizzle, scotch mist, spitting, sheets, cloudburst, showers, downpour, for starters.

So, much as we might rather have a warm, bright day, next time the forecast throws up something that is a little bit unusual, seize this opportunity to go and get properly acquainted!

Freezing rain occurs when the ice crystals in the clouds pass through a band of warmer air, melt into rain, and then plummet through cooler air nearer the ground. If this air is below freezing point, the liquid rain instantly freezes as it lands, coating every surface with a thin layer of ice.

Sleet starts off as snow up in the clouds, where the air is colder. As the flakes of snow fall, rather than growing and crystallising through the damp air below, they begin to partially melt, their form breaking apart into frozen slush. They splatter as they land, breaking the hopeful promise of snow that the clouds above seemed to be holding.

Hail is created when the updraught through thunderclouds sucks water droplets up into colder air. They become supercooled water, and when they meet a tiny particle up in the cloud, they freeze upon contact. As they continue to rise, more water dropiets are captured and create a new, translucent layer on the hailstone. If it passes through an area of water vapour, this creates a layer of opaque white ice. It continues to rise through the thundercloud on the updraught until it cannot be supported any longer. As it falls, it grows some more on its journey down to the ground.

Explore this weather using all your senses. Close your eyes and touch it. Feel how the chill of it begins to numb your fingers. How the wetness, as it melts, pools inside your palm. What happens if you try to scrape it and pile it together? Does it stick? Can you pick up a whole handful? Can you use

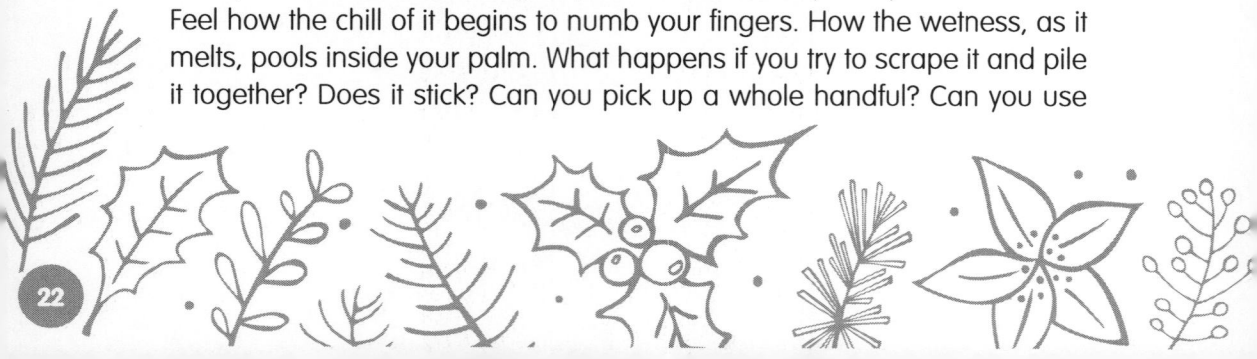

the warmth of your hand to melt the edges enough for them to refreeze together more solidly? You can't smell weather, but it's possible that the rise in humidity that makes precipitation more likely, loosens the mucus layer around your olfactory receptors, allowing your sense of smell to become more acute. Look carefully at it where it has fallen. Can you see any signs of how it was made? What shapes and patterns does it make? Can you hear it when you walk over it? Does it squeak or crunch underfoot? If any has fallen somewhere clean, scrape a little up and taste it.

Accepting

Weather isn't something we can control. No matter how much Hollywood or Christmas cards like to suggest that this time of year is full of blissfully crisp, white snow, the reality is often very different and far more damp and grey. Waiting for the perfect day for the season would mean that we missed out on all the other days, in all their damp, grey glory. The more we can find out about and find something to enjoy in all kinds of weather, the more resilient we will be in life generally, remembering not to waste our life waiting for the better times to come, but finding the glory in what is around us right now.

> Lord, as you surround me with different weather every day, show me also how, as my life changes and swirls around me, your glory is always there, filling my life and my heart.
> Amen.

Journeying

The journey taken by the water droplets in the clouds before we meet them down below is fascinating but hidden. As we stand in freezing rain, squint our eyes against sleet, or take cover from the onslaught of hailstones, we see only the last few moments of that journey. Take a moment to remember, as you are icily splashed, what's been happening in the clouds above you. The water droplets freezing, then melting, forming into hailstones layer upon layer, supercooling through the air, eventually reaching the ground. Their unseen journey shaping the precipitation that

you meet. And that's true for all of us, isn't it. As the quote goes, 'Be kind, for everyone you meet is fighting a battle you know nothing about.' We are all changed by our journeys; sometimes for the better, sometimes it leaves scars. As you meet people today, try to look for glimpses of the journey they've been on. Think of your own. Remember the times of God's grace.

Lord, it is easy to forget that everyone has a past when we only see their present. As we remember the journey of the water droplets in the clouds before ever we meet them on the ground, so help us to remember that each of us has our own journey, and help us to find and cherish those sparkling moments of your grace.
Amen.

WILD
ADVENT

MAKE SNOW TAFFY

Snow is always greeted with excitement by children, and often annoyance by adults. Maybe this is because children see it as another thing to play with and explore, when all adults can see is its potential to disrupt their schedule! There's a wide variety of different types of snowflake, and a seemingly endless variety of shapes and forms within that. Living in London, snow here is definitely a rare treat, especially in any quantities big enough to actually play with, but thanks to the wonders of modern social media I can enjoy snow through the winter vicariously, as I look at photos taken out of other people's windows, and see their children's latest snow creations.

Try placing a little on a dark background – does this give you a better sense of the shape of it, rather than just seeing it all as a white scattering? Maybe you could try drawing it. You'd be in good company – look up Israel Perkins Warren's snowflake classification illustrations.

I read the books of Laura Ingalls Wilder as a child, and loved her stories of pioneering in the wild, wooded areas of the United States long ago. One thing I remember clearly from the books is something they would do when it snowed. It must have been in early spring, when the sap was rising, as it involved maple syrup. They'd go out and tap the trees, collecting the sticky sweet sap in small buckets. Luckily for us, we can just click a button to add maple syrup to our next online delivery! Pour some into a heavy-bottomed saucepan, and boil to about 112° Centigrade, or until it creates a soft ball when dripped into cold water. Scoop up a plateful of clean snow, packing it down to a firm surface. Make sure you don't use a plastic plate. (Here speaks the voice of experience! Boiling maple syrup is HOT! You don't want to melt a hole in your plate.) Very, very carefully, pour the maple syrup over the snow. You can pour it in lines, or like Pa does in *Little House in the Big Woods*, make little pictures with it. Wait for it to cool, and either scoop it up, twiddling it round the prongs of a fork or a lolly stick, or pick it up and pop it in your mouth. Delicious!

Waiting

It's easy to get sucked in to the idea that waiting is a nuisance, something to be avoided, something to be brushed aside as soon as possible. Waiting for a doctor's appointment, waiting for a bus, waiting for a cheque to clear, waiting for the kettle to boil. Perhaps we need to rediscover that overspilling, exuberant anticipation in waiting, that children have about the snow. They know that this is a landmark event. It's not something they can bring about through their own efforts – but it'll change the world as they see it. Are we able to wait in this way for the coming of the Saviour at Christmas?

Lord, as we wait for your coming at Christmas,
change our time of waiting from that of
impatiently marking time, to an attitude
of exuberant anticipation.
Amen.

Birthing

It's rather fun and surprising to make something to eat using ingredients you'd never use in the kitchen. I jumped down a bit of an internet wormhole when I was looking up the temperature to boil the maple syrup to, and discovered a whole world of snow ice-cream. Maybe if the snow lasts long enough, you could experiment with those too! There are times when God's word surprises us, too – no matter how often we hear it, we stumble upon new truths and new wisdom. Psalm 119:103 (NRSV) says, 'How sweet are your words to my taste, sweeter than honey to my mouth!' As you fill your mouth with sweetness, think back over scripture you've heard recently, and reflect on what new sweetness you've discovered in God's word.

Lord, thank you for the surprises and the
sweetness in my life.
Amen.

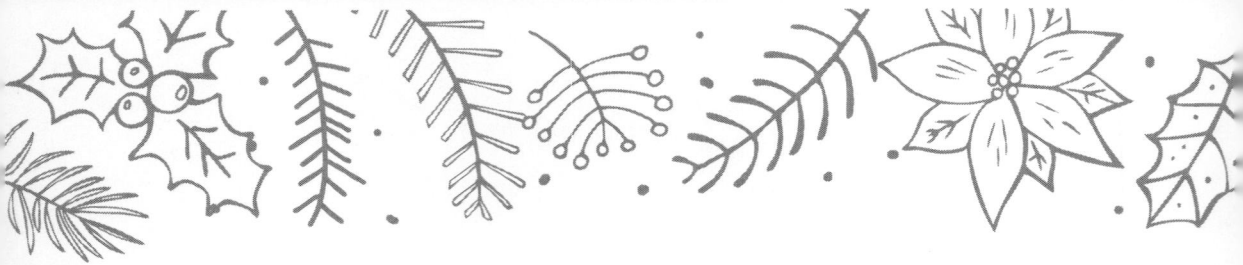

NOTES

THINGS TO DO IN THE DARK

Things to do in the dark...

Make jam-jar lanterns

See page 38

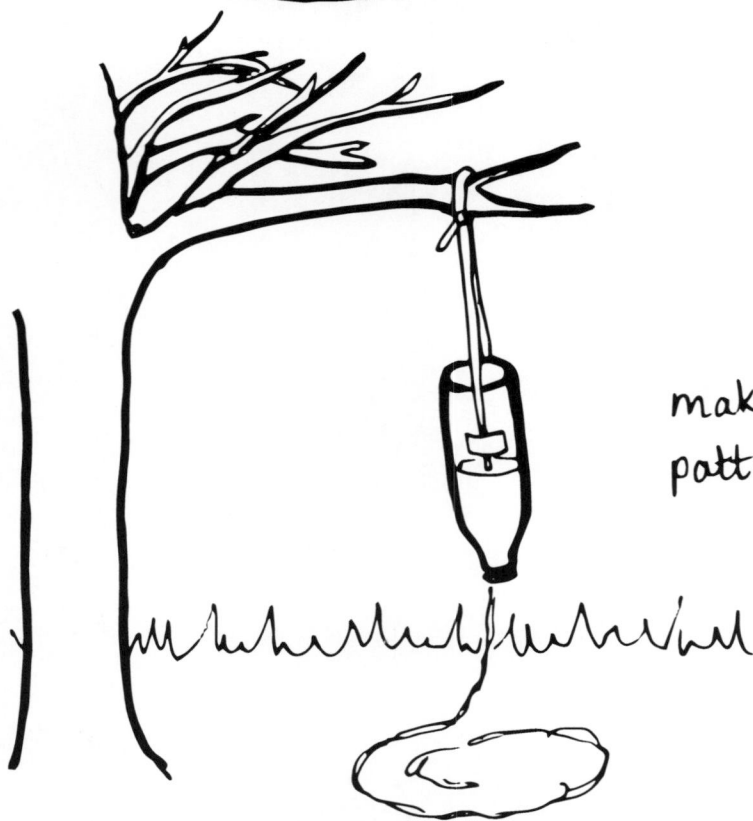

make sand patterns

See page 42

See page 34

make a clay lamp

See page 32

spot when darkness falls

make white pebble patterns

See page 36

SPOT WHEN DARKNESS FALLS

Humans are diurnal creatures – we are awake in the daytime, and sleep at night. Our eyes are excellent at daytime vision, because this is the time we are expected to be using them! The retina at the back of our eye has two types of cells – rods and cones. You have around six million cones which are working all the time when the light is bright enough, giving you fantastic colour vision. You also have around 120 million rods, which you use in the daytime for detecting movement and your peripheral vision, but really come into their own once night starts to fall. As the light levels drop, the cones are no longer able to function. However, the rods can continue working at much lower light levels, giving you a black and white picture of the world.

In Islamic scripture, this is shown by the verse: 'until the white thread appears to you distinct from the black thread'. Scholars have argued that the white thread means dawn, and the black thread means the night, but surely there is something to be said for the way in which increasing light levels change the way our vision works. In the story of creation (Genesis 1:5, NRSV), and in Judaism, each new day starts at dusk, rather than the morning. 'And there was evening and there was morning, the first day.' It's quite a different way to think of a day, with it beginning in this hidden time of darkness rather than with the sun rising, or with the arbitrary ticking over of a clock. Darkness lends itself to reflection. Interesting to think of beginning a new day with this – it might be worth us giving that a go.

This time of year is a fantastic chance to play around with light and darkness. To do so in the summer would require everyone to stay up well past their bedtime (me included by mid-June!), but a simple mid-afternoon walk or outdoor play in December lets you enjoy the dusk without paying the price the next morning. As you walk or as you play, be aware of the gathering darkness. Feel how your eyes are changing; how your vision is changing. Notice as what you see and how you see it changes, and the world shifts from colour to monochrome.

Journeying

As we travel from light into darkness at the end of the day, how we see and what we see changes. Journeying from one place to another often opens your eyes. We acknowledge this openly about visiting different places in the world on holiday, but maybe less often when we think about travelling through time or through experience. Often our view is unchanged but how we see it can be totally revolutionised. We can no less hold back the passage of time or experience than we can hold back the night. However, there is beauty to be found there, and in looking for it and embracing it, our fear of the dark and the unknown vanishes in the wonder of our new vision.

Lord, draw us towards seeing you and your life and goodness, as our vision shifts.
Amen.

Birthing

This nightfall, that you are observing and living through, has never happened before. There have been other nightfalls you may have spent in this place, with these people or alone, in this weather, but this dusk falls new for you today. As you watch the light levels drop, and the view of the world change around you, be aware of the uniqueness of this night. Listen to the sounds around you, feel the air on your skin, and notice the night coming to surround you. What unique newness is coming about in the world because you are here?

Lord, as this new night falls around me, and I am wrapped in its darkness, show me what newness is coming into the world, wrapped up in me.
Amen.

MAKE A CLAY DIVA LAMP

Where I live, there is plenty of clay soil, which is pretty useful for this activity. There's a huge mound of clay on one of my forest school sites. We call it the Clay Volcano, as whenever it rains, the rain pools in the top then cascades down the sides. Hopefully you can find a seam of clay somewhere near you to dig up. If you draw a complete blank on this, you may have to go and find some natural clay to buy, instead. Don't go for the air-dry stuff – that's got tiny plastic fibres inside it to strengthen it, so it's not very good to leave around in the environment.

You need a small lump of clay, enough to fit comfortably inside your hand. Use your thumbs to press it down and shape it into a bowl – a kind of oval/squashed circle shape. Bend up two sides and pinch them together so there's an enclosed centre to the lamp, with two open ends. Cut a length of string, and feed it down one of those openings, into the centre. Pour oil in through the other opening until there's a small pool of it inside. Olive oil or vegetable oil work well, or you can squash in coconut oil.

Carefully light the string wick. It should begin to suck up the oil to feed the little flame – you'll notice that the string itself doesn't burn away as you'd expect, but rather it uses the oil to keep the flame alive. Hold it upright, very carefully, or place it on a flat surface. People have made and used lamps like this for thousands of years to bring a little light into their darkness. They are so simple, but they really work.

Waiting

As you are in the darkness, waiting for the little lamp to be lit, your waiting isn't passive. The thing you are waiting for, the light, is still to come, but your waiting is working towards it. You would be unable to have the light if your waiting didn't involve preparation. This waiting is active. Finding clay, moulding clay, cutting string, pouring oil. It involves cold, muddy hands, your fingers feeling numb and clumsy. It involves you trying out and experimenting with something you may not have done before, or you may not have done for a long time. It involves you taking a risk, trusting that the end result will be worth it, rather than the ease of flipping a switch on a torch.

> Lord, as I wait for your coming at Christmas, let my waiting be active not passive. Give me the courage to experiment, to take risks, and to trust that your light coming into the world will be worth it.
> Amen.

Accepting

This is really a very little lamp. It has limitations. You couldn't use it to light your whole house. It couldn't be used to read a book by, or to light the roads for cars. You need to keep an eye on the level of your oil, or the flame will gutter and go out. If you hold it too enthusiastically, the clay will squash, and (as I know from experience with my eight-year-old) you'll get oil streaks all down your coat that will stay for weeks! If the wind blows too hard, the flame will be extinguished, and it probably wouldn't fare too well in the rain either. But it is still a light in the darkness, and where even the smallest light goes, there darkness vanishes. We can only shine in our own way. We have our limitations. We can't bring light to everyone in every place. But wherever we shine God's love, there darkness vanishes.

> Lord, help me to be part of the light that 'shines in the darkness, and the darkness has not overcome it' (John 1:5, NIV).
> Amen.

PEBBLE PICTURES

It's not just candles that glow in the darkness. If you think about the tale of Hansel and Gretel, they left a trail of white pebbles to follow in the night-time, in order to find their way home. If there were no light at all, obviously you wouldn't be able to see them, but it's the contrasts that show up when light levels are low.

I have a basket of white pebbles for my after-school forest school club in the autumn term, as the nights are drawing in. I scrape aside the leaf litter to reveal the dark earth beneath. The residual glow from the sunset, the far-away street lamps, and the moon is enough to make the white pebbles seem to glow against their dark background.

It's fun to lay them out in different patterns and shapes. You can use them to draw pictures or to write your initial. Maybe you could lay them out in order of size, starting with the smallest and growing bigger and bigger. Some pebbles invite you to use them in a particular way – allow your mind to imagine what they could be made into. If you have someone else with you, you could play a game of Pebble Pictionary – take it in turns to create a picture and see if the other person can guess what you've made. If you don't have anyone else with you, you could take a photo of your creation and send it to someone else to guess.

Accepting

When you make a picture in the daytime you work with colour, choosing shades and tones and brightness. In the darkness, there's not much point having a well-stocked palette. You wouldn't be able to tell the colours apart anyway! When you open your mind to the possibilities within contrast, light, dark, shape and form, you discover a whole new world of picture making. Rather than trying to hold back the darkness, and using up battery life to shine a frustratingly dim light on your work, it's liberating to work with the possibilities that there actually exist in this situation. You may be surprised by how effective this is.

Lord, show me how the things I have, the person I am, can glow within my own situation. Give me the confidence to work within the possibilities that actually exist in my life, and to enjoy what I create.
Amen.

Journeying

Creating a picture using pebbles isn't like drawing with pens or painting with a brush. You can't take the idea inside your head and sweep it out onto paper with your fingers. It's much more of a conversation between you and the pebbles. Sometimes you will suggest the picture; sometimes a pebble will! Sometimes their shapes will put you in mind of something you might create, and at other times you'll be picking up and turning over pebbles to find a shape that will fit the idea you have in your mind. As we decorate the canvas of our lives, it's the people and situations we come up against that will determine what it looks like. Sometimes it'll be our influence changing them, and sometimes it will be their influence changing us. Both are valid and both are important. Influence goes both ways – we shouldn't feel that one side of this is more valuable than the other.

Lord, as we pick up the pebbles, and work with them to make a picture, we reflect on the influences on our lives, and the way we influence the lives of others. We ask that you will fill us with your wisdom to create a future thoughtfully and lovingly with others.
Amen.

JAM–JAR LANTERNS

Tiny tea lights glowing in the darkness are a magical sight, but one which it doesn't take much more than a breath of wind to snuff out. Give that a try now. Light your tea light outside, and see how difficult it is for it to maintain a flame in the lightest breeze. What's needed is something to protect the little flame from the force of the wind. Something that will still let the light shine through.

In short, you want a jam jar. A perfectly formed, readily accessible, mass-produced tea light holder, sometimes masquerading as a temporary home for sweet condiments on toast! You could just pop the tea light inside, and that would do the job. I find if I try to light the tea light from above, I end up burning my fingers on the match. Far easier to light the tea light, hold it by its edges, then drop it into the jam jar.

It's nicer still to decorate the jam jar. Although many autumn leaves are well on their way to becoming leaf mulch by this point in the year, you can probably find a good selection of leaves of different colours and shapes. Use a glue stick or clear sticky tape to attach them to the outside of your jam jar. As the candle glows through the leaves, it'll bring out their shapes and colour, and cast lovely shadows. The glass of the jar may get hot as the candle burns, so either place it on a safe surface, or tie a string securely under the lip, and a loop for hanging off that.

Waiting

The tea light candle by itself, lit outdoors on a winter's evening, isn't going to last long. You need to hold off with the match until you've got a lantern ready for it to shelter in. What shelter is it you are waiting for in your life before you are able to burn as brightly as you should? Psalm 46:1 (Good News) reminds us that 'God is our shelter and strength, always ready to help in times of trouble.' Take some time to give thanks for the shelter God has provided for you in your life thus far, and to notice the places of shelter and safety in your life now, which will help you shine.

Lord, thank you for providing me with shelter
in times of trouble, and giving me the strength
to shine.
Amen.

Accepting

The patterns of the shadows cast by the leaves and other natural objects
you've attached to the outside of your jam jar flicker over the surface the jam
jar is placed on. Beautiful as a steady glow is, this ever-moving, constantly-
changing pattern of shapes and colours is more special. How lovely that
it's the pattern of our light and our dark times that join together to form the
pattern of our days, and grow into the pattern of our time on earth. We may
long for the steady glow of easy brightness, but looking back we can see
some blessings too, even in our dark times.

Lord, thank you for taking the dark times and the
bright times of my life, and weaving both of them
into a rich, textured story of a life lived within
your love.
Amen.

USING YOUR SENSES

Around 80 to 85 per cent of how we understand and make sense of the world comes through sight. It is by far and away our most important and well-used sense. It's no surprise that we find ourselves lost and uncomfortable in the dark, and fear of the dark is incredibly common amongst small children. Things look different. Our imagination begins to play tricks on us, turning a bush into a terrifying creature, a lump on a tree trunk into an assailant lying in wait to attack us. Our imagination never seems to use the dark to trick us into believing the things we half see are pleasant, does it!

As dark falls tonight, try stilling yourself outside. Slow your breathing down, so your brain isn't tricked into believing you're under threat. Notice yourself breathing in the dark night air, holding it for a moment, then letting it go, back out into the night. As you stand or sit enclosed in the darkness, begin to notice the sounds around you. This isn't a test of how many nature sounds you can identify by heart, although you may have some that you know. It isn't a judgement on whether you actually have nature sounds around you, either. In my garden I'm as likely to hear the sound of sirens as much as anything! What you might notice, though, is that the night sounds are different from the day sounds. The birds have gone quiet – no singing, no flapping, only occasional rustling from their roosts. Night sounds in December are different from the summer too – no snuffling hedgehogs or mating foxes tonight. You may hear an owl, or geese flying overhead.

Use your hands to feel the night around you. It's surprising how you notice the roughness of the bark when you can't see it, or how smooth holly leaves are in between their prickles. Feel the night lying damply on the ground, and smell it in the air. You might catch the smell of smoke from a woodburner stove or a fireplace. In the darkness your other senses heighten. You become aware of more than just what there is to see, and know it in more depth, in more intimacy.

Accepting

Night is not like day. There are things you can't do and can't see. A damp, cold winter night is not like a balmy summer night, either. Where a summer

night is full of warmth and life, a winter's night can feel almost hostile. For naked apes like ourselves, it's a time when we need shelter for our survival. Living in our comfortable homes, we unsurprisingly dash quickly through the gloom at the end of the winter's day to get inside, where we'll be warm and safe. Maybe our ancestors also rushed through this alien world to get safely inside their huts, their shelters and their caves. But spending some time to acquaint ourselves with this dark world means we are able to really inhabit it, rather than see it as somewhere just to pass through. As we try to dash quickly through the uncomfortable and dark things in our lives through to a safe shelter, maybe we need to remember the words of Psalm 139 verse 12 (NRSV) – 'Even the darkness is not dark to you; the night is as bright as the day, for darkness is as light to you.'

Lord, you are intimately acquainted with the things in my life I keep hidden, as well as the things I share. Help me to still myself and spend some time this Advent exploring my dark and hidden places in your company, and learning to love the person I find.
Amen.

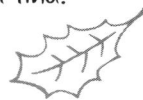

Birthing

That 20 or 15 per cent of your senses, lying underused and underdeveloped, gets some practice when you're out in the dark. The more you use them, the more you notice, and the better honed your senses will be. What other underused skills have you been able to exercise this Advent? What underdeveloped talents have you been able to bring to birth in this lead-up to the birth of Jesus at Christmas?

Lord, I give you thanks for all my skills and talents, the obvious and the hidden. Help me to discover, to use, and to develop those hidden skills and talents of mine, to your glory.
Amen.

KINETIC GRAVITY SAND ART

White sand shows up really well in the dark, on top of dark soil. For this activity, you're going to allow the sand to draw patterns all by itself, with just the assistance of gravity. Kick and scrape away any leaf litter on the ground under a tree to reveal the dark winter earth. Because of the time of year, there shouldn't be any little green shoots poking out – the earth will be a dark, blank canvas.

Repurpose an old plastic bottle to help you create your art by poking a hole in the lid, filling it with sand, and screwing the lid back on. Attach string to each side of the bottle with strong sticky tape, and hang it over a branch. Keep your finger over the hole in the lid as you do so, or your sand will start pouring out before you're ready to create your picture.

Once it's securely attached to the tree, above the dark soil, give the bottle a swing or a push. Gravity will pull the sand out of the hole in the bottle, down onto the dark soil floor. Gravity will also act on the bottle, affecting its course as it swings like a pendulum. This will create ellipse patterns on the ground. Because the sand is so pale against the dark earth, even in low light levels you'll be able to enjoy it. And because sand, unlike other free-flowing substances (paint or salt, for example), is naturally found in soil, a little extra won't affect the natural environment too much. If your sand is very fine, you may find you need to screen your art canvas area from the wind, which is easy enough to do if you've got some spare hands to hold a tarpaulin in a useful position.

Waiting

To make a picture in the dark, playing on the use of contrast, of a light colour on a dark one, you need to first prepare your canvas. Prepare the ground. Leaf litter will have built up over the weeks and the months of autumn, rotting down in the dampness. The leaf litter from previous years will have become rich, dark earth. To provide a space for your art to take place, you need to clear the loose stuff away, scraping with the side of your foot until only the dark earth shows through. As we wait through Advent

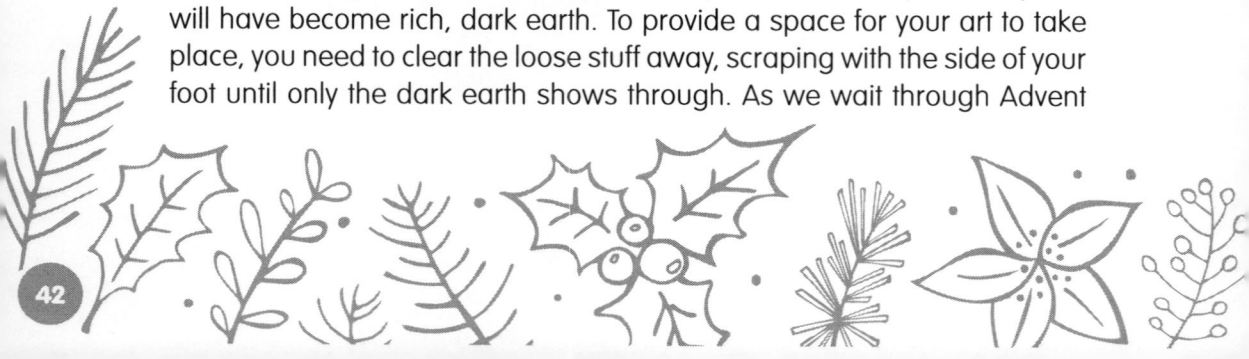

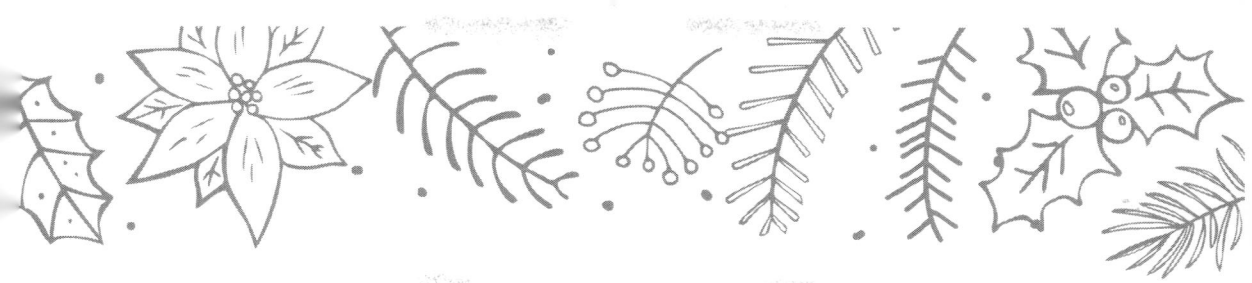

for the coming of our Saviour, born among us at Christmas, how are we preparing the ground, how are we preparing the canvas ready for what he will create in our lives?

> Lord, as I clear the ground, show me what I need to clear away in my life, as I wait for your coming at Christmas.
> Amen.

Journeying

Watching the sand trickle out from the bottle as it swings, forming marks on the dark earth, is mesmerising. A seemingly random swing turns into purposeful patterns as forces outside our control act on the suspended bottle. Gravity pulls the chaos of our swing into beautiful order. As we trace the pattern of our life's journey, can we see times when the force of God's love has pulled the chaos of our lives into a pattern of order and beauty? As we travel through this Advent, let us keep our senses attuned to feel the pull of this force of perfect love on our lives.

> Lord, as I watch the invisible force of gravity working on the bottle and the sand within it, draw my attention to the invisible force of your love, working on my life.
> Amen.

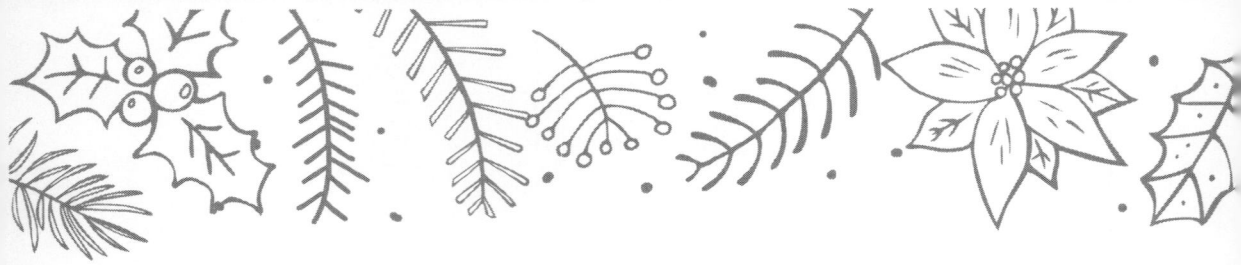

NOTES

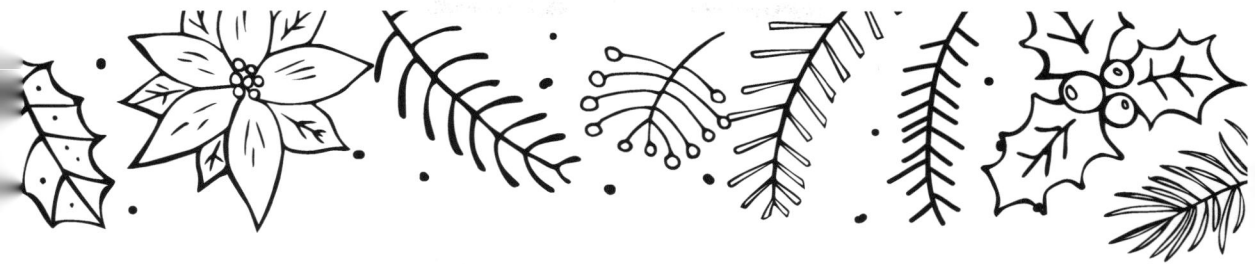

THINGS TO DO WITH OTHERS

Things to do with others...

make a shadow theatre

See page 56

toast marshmallows on a Yule bonfire

See page 50

lie on blankets and look at the stars

See page 52

set up
a trail
of light,
leading to
a hot chocolate
bar

See
page
48

have an outdoor candlelit dinner

See
page
58

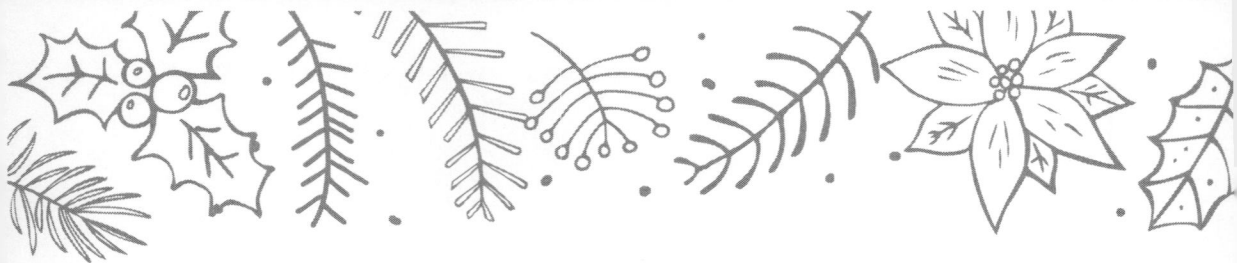

TRAIL OF LIGHT

Imagine arriving at an agreed destination, wrapped up warm against the cold of the evening, and following a trail of tea lights, their light pooling against the ground and the trees' branches showing you a path, to find a galaxy of tea lights in jam jars, flasks of hot chocolate, mulled wine or mulled cider, and good friends.

This is the kind of thing that's as fun to set up as it is to take part in. You may need to eat your way through your glut of late-autumn jam first (or you could take the less tasty route, and ask around for empty jam jars from friends or freecycle). Find somewhere you would be able to lay your trail. Make sure it's somewhere that you'll feel safe in the evening. I can think of places round here that are fine in the day but the evening is out of bounds. Make sure it's somewhere with a decent kind of pathway so you are able to create an interesting route. Before darkness falls completely – or you could just bring a large torch – lay the trail, placing jam jars at intervals along the path, and making sure that any ambiguous points are clearly marked so you don't lose your visitors!

Choose a space at the end of the trail to spread picnic blankets on the ground, and you could hang tea light lanterns from the branches too, here. If you don't have specific tea light lanterns, you can tie string round the top of a jam jar to make a hanging handle. The more lights in this spot, the more magical it will feel. If you can find a log or two to act as your 'bar' for hot chocolate, mulled wine, or mulled cider, that'll make it a clearer focus and stop people tripping over the flasks. Let your friends know when to arrive and where, and tell them to follow the trail of lights, then sit back and wait for them to appear.

Waiting

Setting up something like this can be a bit of an enterprise. You'll end up with a to-do list, a shopping list, maybe persuading your kids to leave their warm house with their screens inside it, maybe wrestling your toddler into warm overtrousers when they'd rather wear their princess dress, maybe

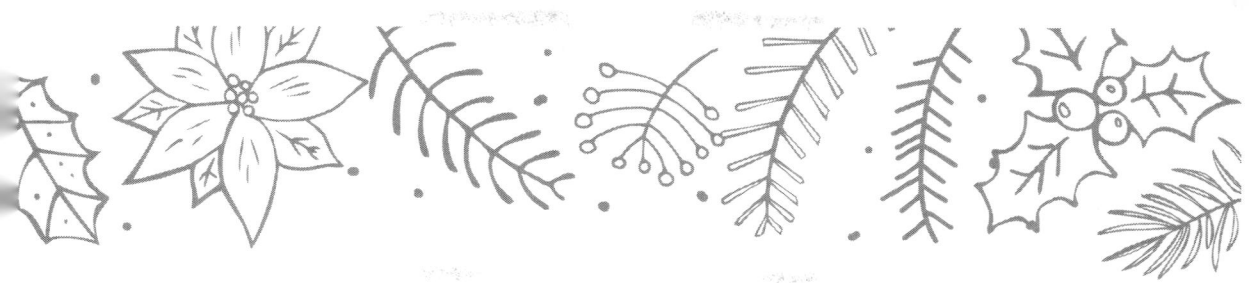

a last-minute dash to the shops when you realise you've already run out of hot chocolate powder. Not unlike our preparations for Christmas itself, really. And yet, eventually, you'll end up with no more to do, and no more to prepare, just waiting in the clearing, surrounded by candles, for your friends to appear. That anticipation in the waiting is something we could maybe do with capturing as we wait for Jesus at Christmas.

> Lord, amongst our busyness and preparations, help us to wait for Jesus at Christmas with anticipation. Amen.

Journeying

Stepping out into the darkness to travel along a path, you have to trust to your feet. You have to look ahead to the next way point, and often can't see any further ahead than that. You travel one step at a time, trusting that the next part of your path will become apparent as you get there. Often, when we set out on a journey we have the route planned in advance. Our satnav will give us the optimum route, and we are even able to use the internet before we leave to see what our destination will look like. There's a lot we can learn about trust from following a candle-lit trail like this.

> Lord, I trust you to be the lamp for my feet and a light to my path. Amen.

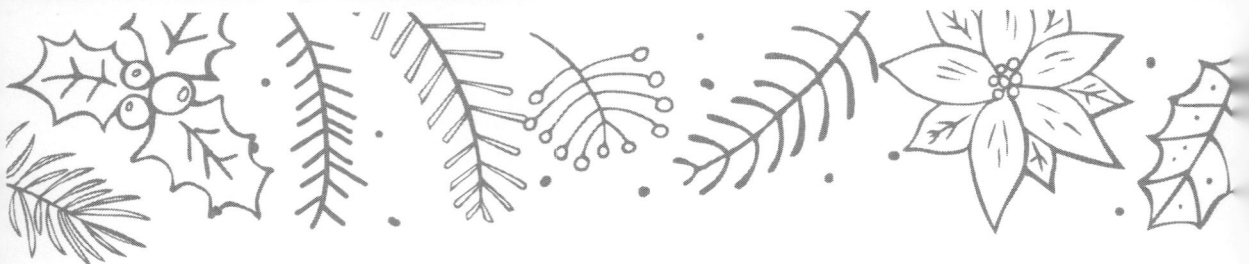

SHADOW THEATRE

Take advantage of the early evenings, and make a shadow theatre. You'll need a white sheet, some clothes pegs, a rope or length of paracord, a strong electric light, and some lumps of rock or logs. Tie the rope or paracord between two trees, a couple of metres apart, and make sure it's tied good and taut, so the sheet doesn't start to sag. Peg the sheet along the rope, and hold it down at the bottom with the lumps of rock or logs. Find somewhere to hang your electric light a short distance away behind the sheet. I've used what seems to be referred to as a DIY work light, which has an array of LEDs rather than just a strong point of light.

If you place yourself between the light and the sheet, you'll cast a shadow that people standing in front of the sheet will be able to see. When we did this at the forest school after-school club in the winter, the kids really loved creating crazy shows for us to watch.

Maybe you can remember how to make your hands into shadow puppets – I can normally manipulate mine to be a crocodile, a bird, and some vague approximation of a dog. Looking online, there are loads of ideas for things you can make your hand shadows become. Or you could use natural objects to create a shadow puppet – a blob of clay stuck on a stick is a good starting point for you to then poke other bits and pieces into.

Accepting

Shadows aren't often the thing we're wanting to create. We seldom notice shadows, with our attention drawn rather to the actual physical things in front of us. When we do think of shadows, it's often in a negative way – a dark and gloomy passing over, restricting our access to the light, or to joy and happiness. But shadows can also be something to be cherished. Think of sitting beneath a shady tree in the heat of the summer. These shadows you are making tonight are brilliantly creative, too.

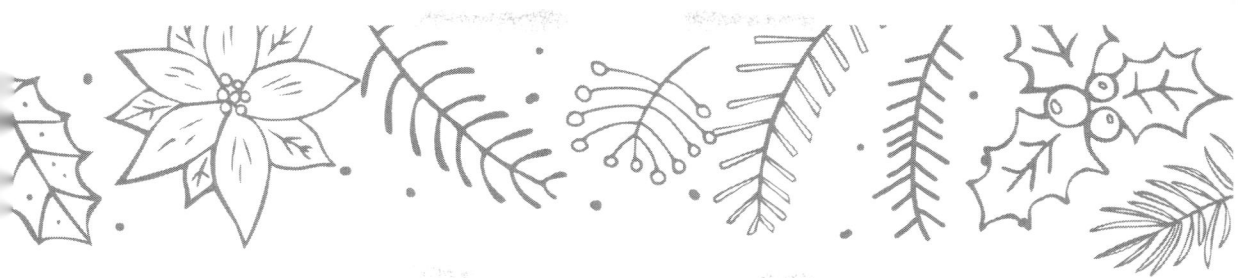

Lord, you are with me in the bright times, and in the shadowy times. Open my eyes to the things I should cherish within my times of shadow.
Amen.

 **Birthing**

When you are cavorting behind the sheet, it's hard to imagine what shadows your body is throwing. You can twist your hand into a shape that looks like a creature, but in shadow form it looks nothing like. Sometimes, though, a surprising movement, or an unlikely position creates something brilliant for your spectators to watch. You hear their reactions, and you use that to shape what it is you're doing. Sometimes when we're bringing things to birth, God calls us to step out in faith, to try things out, to experiment. It's no bad thing to try things, and to change things, keeping an ear out always to pinpoint when we're doing things right.

Lord, help me listen, to experiment, and to be willing to change as I go, while I get involved in godly creation.
Amen.

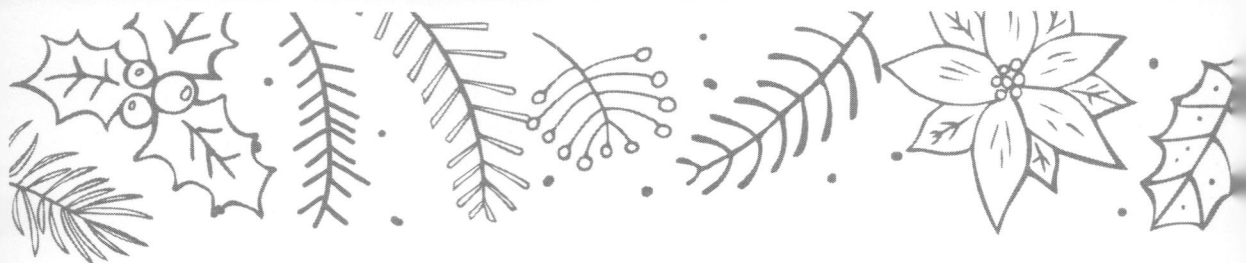

STAR–GAZING ON A BLANKET

If you can find an evening without too much cloud cover, you'll be able to enjoy the night sky. The lack of clouds will mean it's going to be a cold night, so make sure you wear enough layers to stay warm as you lie still outside. I'm talking thermal vests, long johns, an extra jumper (I rely on my trusty poncho under my coat), gloves, a hat, maybe an extra pair of socks or your woollen socks, home-knitted for you by your auntie. It might be worth bringing a flask of soup to share, so that you can warm up with something warm inside you when you start chilling off.

Spread out a waterproof picnic blanket on the ground. Pile on some extra blankets to wrap up in if you can carry them to your star-gazing site. When star-gazing with other people, it feels less lonely to lie down like spokes of a wheel, with your heads all meeting in the middle, otherwise you'll be trying to chat with someone's muddy boot. Wait a while, gazing up into space, for your night vision, and see how many stars you start to spot.

I do know some constellations off by heart, but mostly rely on a star chart app on my phone. Be a little careful with phone use in the dark, as it doesn't take long for your eyes to lose their adjustment to the dark. I've really enjoyed getting to know some of the stars by name: Sirius, Vega, Castor and Pollux. The Geminid meteor shower peaks in mid-December, too, so you may get lucky and find the sky puts on a show for you. No matter how hard you find it to spot pinpricks of light in the sky, you'll manage to spot the moon, and to wonder at how it maybe was once part of our planet, how it's the only other place in space that humans have walked, how their footsteps are still there, imprinted on the dust.

A word about light pollution. There are places designated as dark sky reserves, which will give you an awesome show of the night sky. You may not be in a position to get to one of these just for one of your Advent activities, though. Looking at the night sky is possible wherever you are – you may just have to adjust your expectations. We live in London; my small son gave a happy sigh one evening as he spotted the red glow of the sky at night. Here was I, feeling frustrated at the lack of stars, but he was looking in wonder at the night sky he loved.

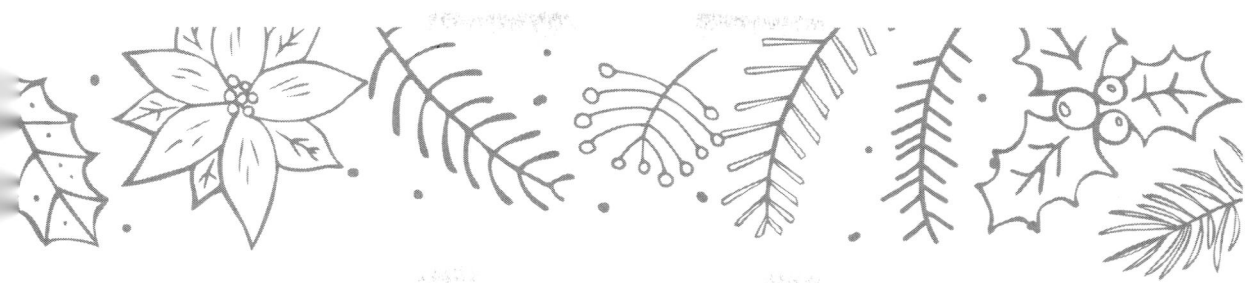

Something else to do, as you lie there on your blanket gazing up, is to remember that celestially there is no up or down. It's all just gravitational attraction. Exercise your mind and imagine yourself gazing out into space, and then even down into space. Each is equally as true. Feel the glue of gravity sticking you onto the skin of your home planet, so that you don't drop off, down, down, down into that sea of stars below you.

Waiting

There's a lot of waiting that goes on when you're star-gazing. Waiting for the clouds to clear. Waiting for the first star of the evening. Waiting while the earth turns. It's easy to forget that the biggest wait of all is over. The light you are seeing now was created a long time back in the past. Our closest star (apart from the sun) created the light you see on earth over four years ago. The light from other stars in our galaxy was made tens of thousands of years ago. Light from stars we see in other galaxies started its journey to earth millions of years ago. There are some far-away stars that are so distant that the light left them billions of years ago. It's completely possible that some of the stars you are seeing, no longer exist. You are looking back in time. Take heart from the unnoticed waiting you have already completed. Let the stars settle you and your waiting into a better sense of perspective.

> Lord, sometimes waiting can be agonising, painful, and worrying. Help me to see my waiting within the vast expanse of your time.
> Amen.

Accepting

There may be footprints on the moon, but they are not my footprints. There are stars and planets out there, too many to number, which neither I nor my descendants will ever visit. The stars are burning, the planets are spinning,

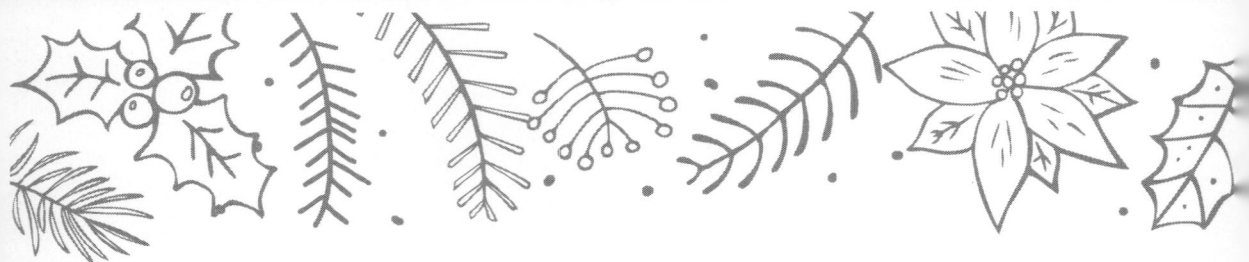

all without any influence on my part. Read Psalm 8:3-5 to yourself as you lie and gaze into the depths of space. No matter how small this expanse may make you feel, you are still loved and precious.

Lord, all too often I measure my worth by what I do, by how much influence I have. Let your stars and planets remind me that I am infinitely small, but that my worth to you isn't measured by what I do, but by the simple fact that you love me. Amen.

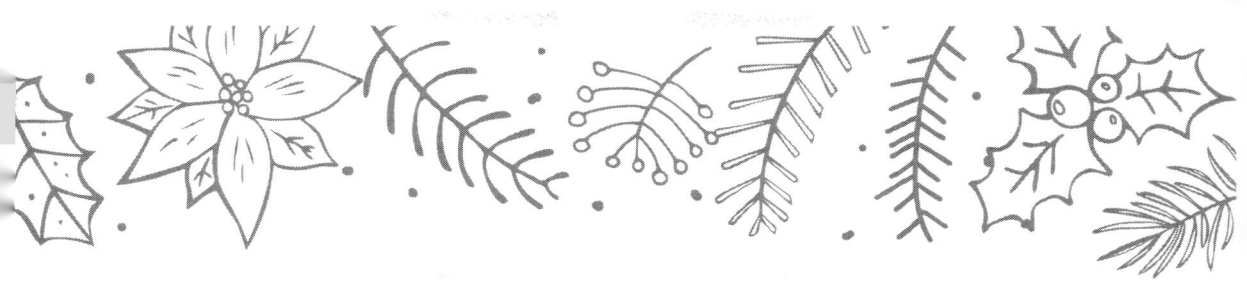

WILD
ADVENT

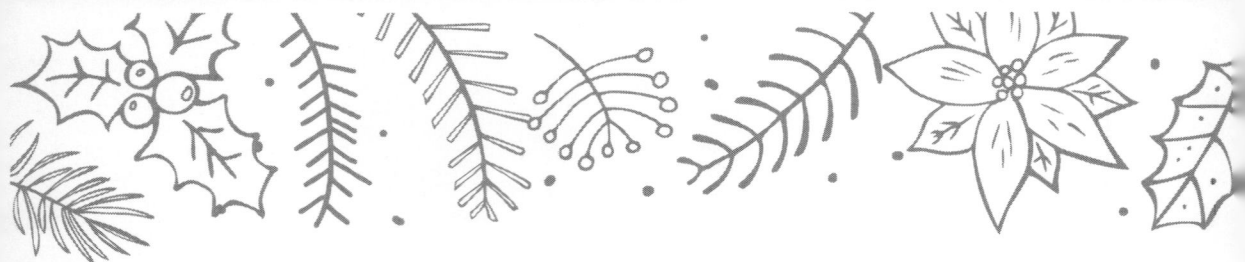

YULE BONFIRE

The feast of Yule has been celebrated in this country for thousands of years, as a midwinter festival around the time of the winter solstice. The winter solstice occurs at the longest night of the year, around 21 December. Traditionally, people would gather to celebrate this turning point of the year, the point at where it is so dark it will get no darker, the point at where light will begin to be reborn into the world.

People would celebrate with night after night of feasting. You may well not have time in your busy pre-Christmas calendar for this, and besides which, there's something to be said for keeping this as a mini-Lent, preparing ourselves for the feast of Christmas. But a night's feasting amongst friends will give you a foretaste of the Christmas feasting to come, and help to bond you amongst a sense of community.

Collect wood for a bonfire. If you've left a pile, check it carefully before you light it for hibernating hedgehogs, insects and toads. If you're using waste wood, make sure it hasn't been treated with anything that will envelop your guests in toxic fumes! Remind your guests of how to behave around a fire. Make sure there's a metre around your fire pit kept clear, that there are obvious exit routes in case your fire gets out of control, that you keep a bucket of water to hand. It might be sensible to have a rule where only a named adult adds stuff to the fire – if children want to help, they can collect wood and pass it to the adult to put it on the fire. That helps build a sense of purposeful community, anyway.

It's nice to have stuff to eat together that you can only have when you have a fire. Toasted marshmallows, obviously. And toasted starburst sweets for vegetarians/vegans (they're ok in the UK but the recipe is different in different countries, so check your own context). Slices of apple, dipped in sugar, and toasted on sticks is nice. Damper bread is where you mix flour and milk to a soft dough, squash it onto sticks, and hold it over the fire until it cooks. Wrap sweetcorn in foil and leave it in the embers.

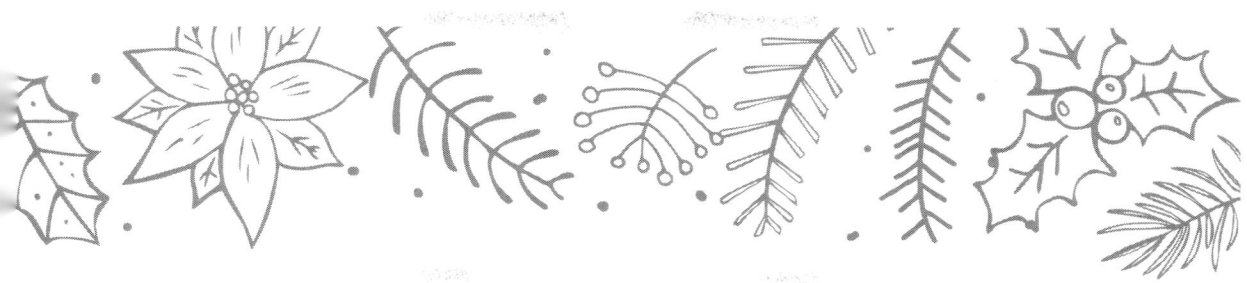

Journeying

There's a real sense of reaching a pivotal point in our journey around the sun at this time of year. The days have got shorter and shorter until it feels as if we'll never see daylight again. The darkness is a good time for self-reflection, remembering our last year's journey, the things we've been and done while travelling round the sun over the past year. Bringing together a group for a bonfire also helps us reflect on our journey together as a community. How some friendships stretch back a long way, and how others are just beginning.

> Lord, I remember my past year with all its joys and sorrows. I give thanks for the communities I am part of, and the relationships just beginning to grow. Amen.

Birthing

What turns a gathering of people into a party? Is it a shared reason for being there? Is it the food and drink? You can collect a group of people in a train carriage, or waiting at a bus stop, and that's not a party. Although, sometimes, often when things go wrong, the magic happens. People begin to talk together, to share, and to smile. Gathering this group in the darkness around your yule fire, there's magic that happens here. Friendships are made and deepened. Children spill out of the pool of firelight, creating their own worlds of half-imagination in the darkness. As the fire is fed, the able-bodied collect two hot drinks and pass one to someone unsteady on their feet. Amongst the organisation, don't miss a chance to stand and enjoy watching how this group of people are, thanks to you, a community.

> Lord, you draw us together and make us one. Amen.

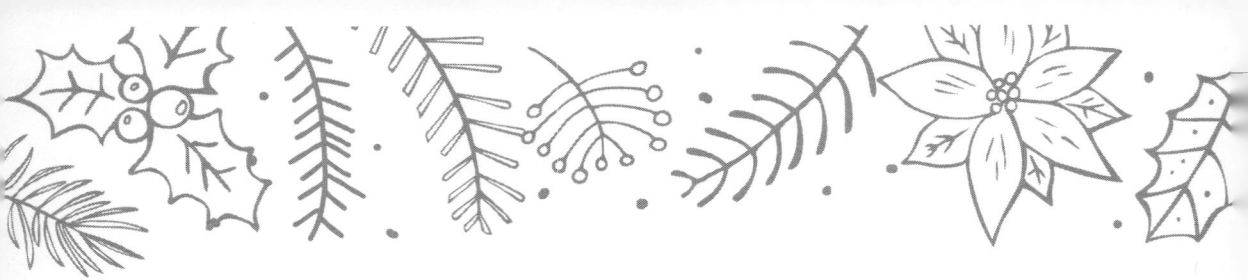

CANDLELIT DINNER

A candlelit dinner doesn't have to be kept solely for romantic couples. Sure, you'll have a few more challenges preparing a candlelit dinner outside for a group of you in a cold dark December evening, but what's life without a challenge?

Think of food you can eat fast, that will stay hot, that's not too fussy. You don't want to be picking your way through a chilly salad trying to catch it on your fork as it blows around in the wind. Think too of what you serve it in. Food spread out over a flat plate will cool down much faster than food in a deep bowl. Think about providing your dinner guests with blankets and maybe hot water bottles or those wheat bags you put in the microwave. I have been known to sit outside in chilly drizzle wrapped up in a back-to-front picnic blanket – blanket side next to me, waterproof layer facing the rain!

We've got a picnic table in our garden. It gets well used throughout the summer but sits there unused and unloved once the weather starts to turn gloomy. There's a large picnic table down on the marshes locally, which we only ever use in the summer, too. This is a great opportunity to reclaim them and enjoy them. Pop your candles inside a jam jar, or use storm lamps so they won't blow out in the wind. Enjoy snatching the chance to eat together, to eat outside, to enjoy candlelight in the darkness. Your guests may think you're crazy but I guarantee you'll be glad you've bothered.

Accepting

Eating outside in Britain is often a matter of struggling against the elements, and has a faint sense of risk and danger! The classic picture of a summer bbq has someone huddled under an umbrella, patiently turning the sausages. We once had a truly epic birthday picnic in June – just as well I'd brought a tarp to sling up between the trees. We just about managed to rescue the birthday cake from the downpour. There's still something that compels us to eat outside, though, and it's the kind of thing that family memories are made of. It creates an attitude where we can enjoy all kinds of weather, rather than just waiting for the perfect warm sunny day, and this is a good message to take into the rest of life, too, isn't it.

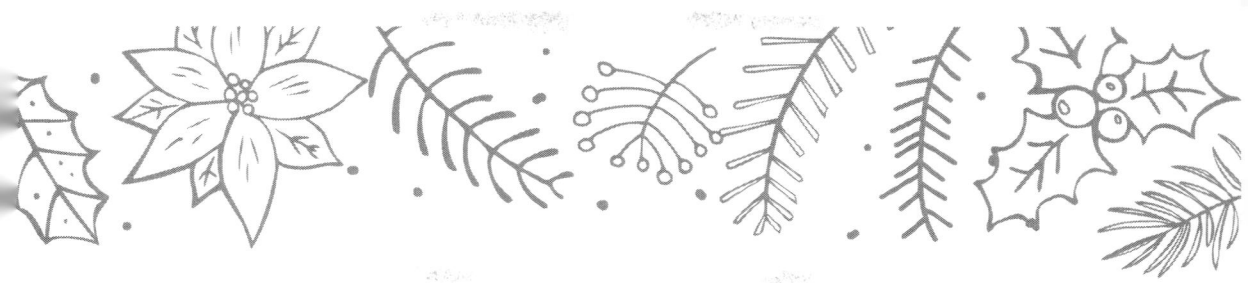

Lord, rather than wait for perfection before I can enjoy the life you've given me, help me to try to actively seek out your goodness in all situations. Amen.

Journeying

Sitting in the garden eating your dinner, in the cold and the dark, doesn't seem much of a journey. You're stationary, after all. But you're taking yourself on a journey, pushing the boundaries of what is deemed acceptable and normal. You're journeying through being a little uncomfortable, and finding ways to keep yourself warmer. You're journeying through ways of lighting your meal, as your tea light blows out and you find a new solution. You're journeying as your body, warm from the indoors, begins to chill slowly but surely, as your internal heating system battles against the temperature outdoors. Be attentive to how you almost without thinking make small adjustments for your comfort, tucking your blanket a little tighter, pulling up your hood. A journey can be made up of those micro-changes.

Lord, as I travel towards Christmas, help me little by little to adjust my thoughts and my actions to follow you better. Amen.

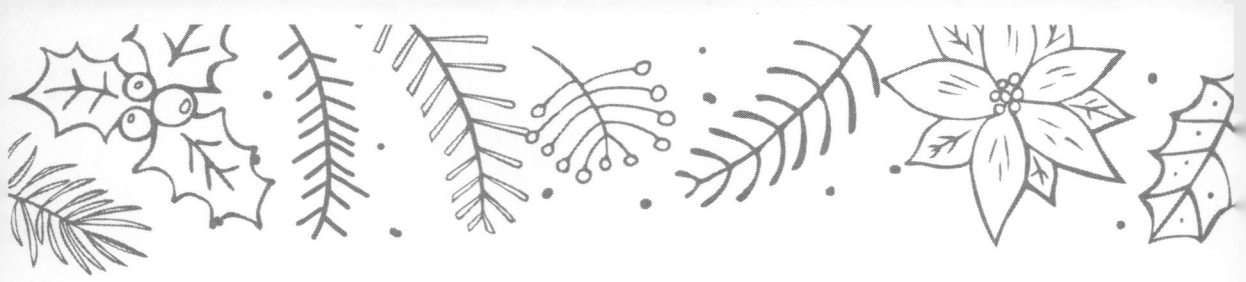

NOTES

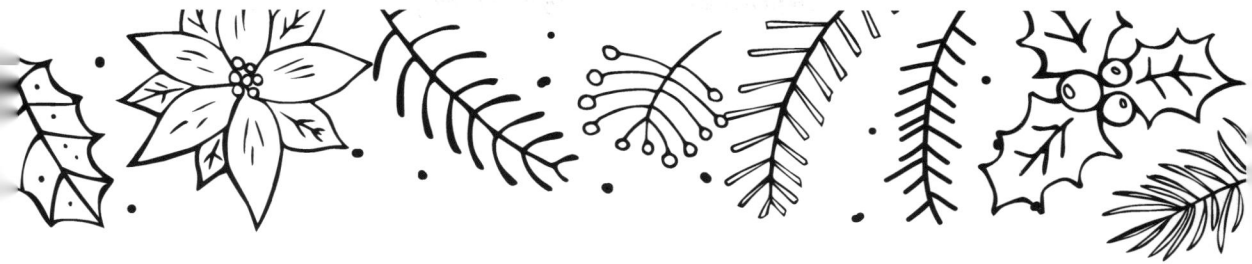

SHORT AND EASY THINGS TO MAKE AND DO

Short and easy things to make + do...

make bird feeders

See page 72

See page 64

light a fire

make a nativity scene

See page 68

make a wreath

See page 74

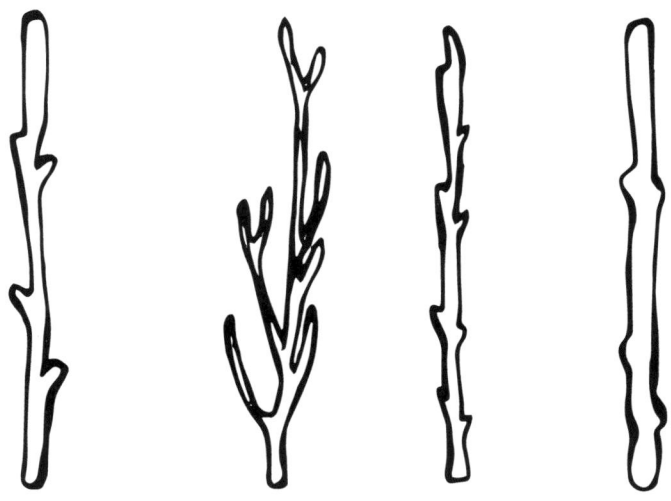

identify sticks

See page 70

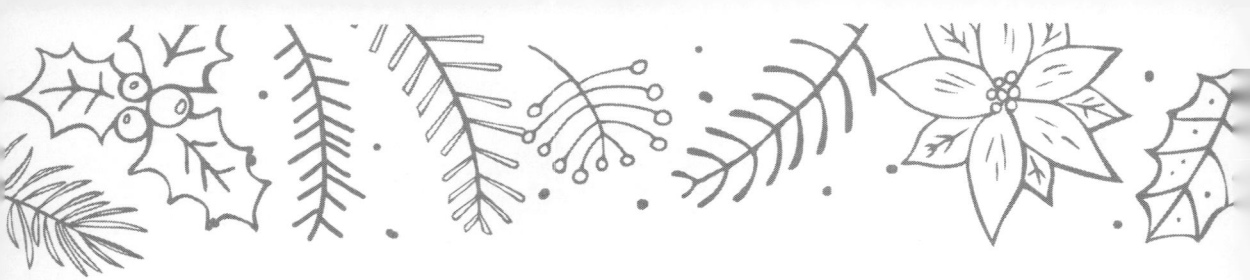

FIRE-LIGHTING

Poking around with a fire has to be one of the most pleasurable things you can do. Fire has been many things to us as a species: safety, warmth, food, a focus for companionship at the end of a day, and a backdrop to a sharing of communal story. There has been a huge resurgence of people owning wood-burning stoves, as they seek to recapture that warmth, both physical and psychological, of having a fire in the house.

If you own a stove, you may well be an expert at fire-laying and fire-lighting already, and I'm speaking to the converted. If you don't, you may remember afternoons in the garden with your grandpa burning the garden waste, or that wet holiday in a cottage, twisting newspaper and crossing your fingers that this match will take. There's nothing like coaxing a flame into being.

I'm going to suggest that you go right back to basics. Rather than start with a match or a lighter, spend some time teaching yourself to catch a flame from a spark. You can buy a steel fire striker pretty cheaply from most shops that have an 'outdoor' section (or online, obviously). You need one of those with two parts held together by string – one metal cylinder, and one flat striker. To get a spark, you draw the striker firmly over the surface of the metal cylinder, fairly briskly. After a few attempts, you should get a scattering of sparks. This is exciting stuff! No good, though, to scatter those sparks on nothing. Fluffed-up cotton wool catches a spark really well; if you want to go totally natural, you may still be able to find some fluffy seed heads, or King Alfred's cake fungus.

Once you've succeeded in getting your spark to catch, and grow a flame, you'll need some fuel to turn that into a fire. Find a safe place for your fire, maybe a fire pit or an old biscuit tin, well away from anything flammable. Sort through your fuel, organising by thickness. Be fussy here; the more finely graded your fuel, the easier you'll find it to get your fire going. Birch twigs are particularly good, as is birch bark, as it contains oils that help the flame to 'take'. I like a 'waffle lay' when I set out my sticks. Lay your thickest sticks on the bottom layer, side by side. Lay your next thickest on top, at a ninety-degree angle. And so on, until you have the thinnest,

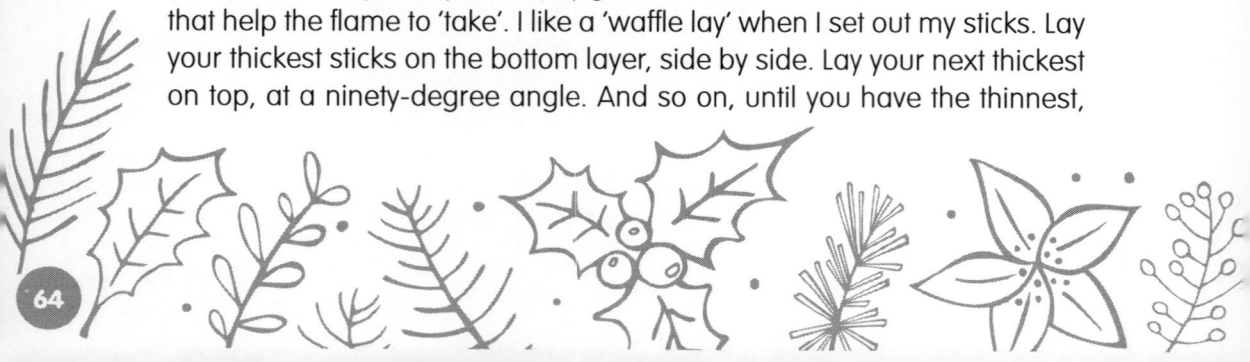

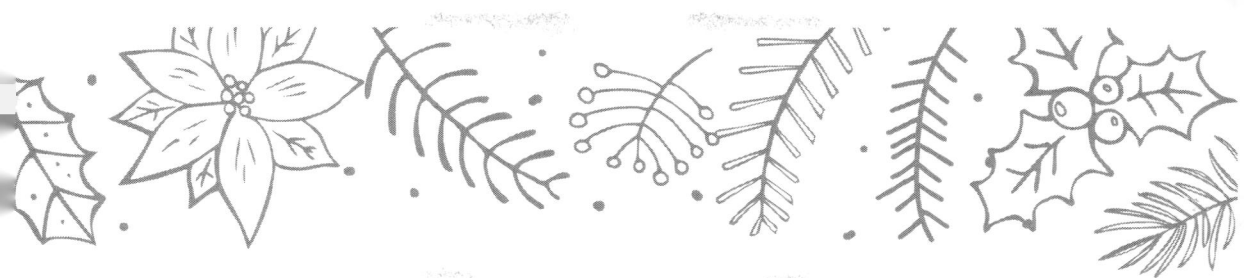

twiggiest twigs on the top. I like to finish this with a good clump of birch bark (my kids get embarrassed when I pocket it on the school run, but the council planners did help me out with a good couple of streets full of silver birch!), and then the well-fluffed cotton wool on top of it all. You may need to feed the flame on the cotton wool with some of your bark, but soon the fire should take hold and begin to work its way through your fuel stack, and you can sit back and enjoy (or kneel and blow and prod and fiddle, if you're anything like me; that's half the fun!).

Accepting

Working with a fire teaches you to work within your limitations. It is all immediate, and a fire is a little like a needy toddler, who wants all your attention and wants it now. With the best will in the world, you can create the most awesome pile of neatly sorted sticks, and a brilliant tinder pile, but then events overwhelm you. The bark you tried fizzles up too fast; the sticks you thought would be just right you suddenly discover to be too damp. You reach into your pile and find the best fit; the fuel that is needed for just this time and this moment. There's no point wishing for that other handful of birch twigs you nearly picked up in the park the other day. What you have has to be enough, and somehow you make it enough. We may feel that what we have to offer is inadequate, but somehow God makes it enough.

Lord, teach me to work with what I have, and take what I can offer and use it to your glory. Amen.

Birthing

Making a fire is the ultimate in making something from nothing. You create this thing that feels almost alive, that moves, and breathes, and consumes. It is, of course, also the ultimate in making nothing from something. You start with a pile of sticks, and end up with nothing but a little ash. However, as we all know from school science lessons, the law of conservation of energy reminds us that both those statements are untrue. We have rather taken the energy stored in the wood, and changed it into heat and light (and a bit of

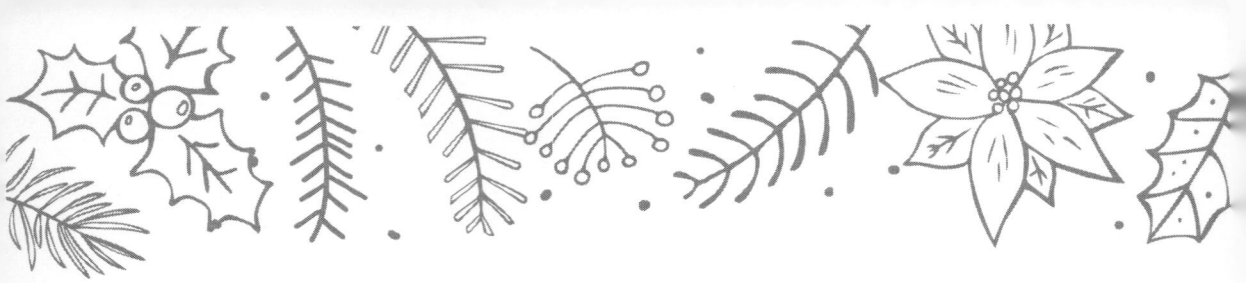

a crackling noise). What energy is stored in you, through your experiences, your talents, and your personality? Is there a way you are being called to change it from something stored to something shared?

Lord, help me to unlock the energy and potential stored inside myself, so that I can blaze with your love and life.
Amen.

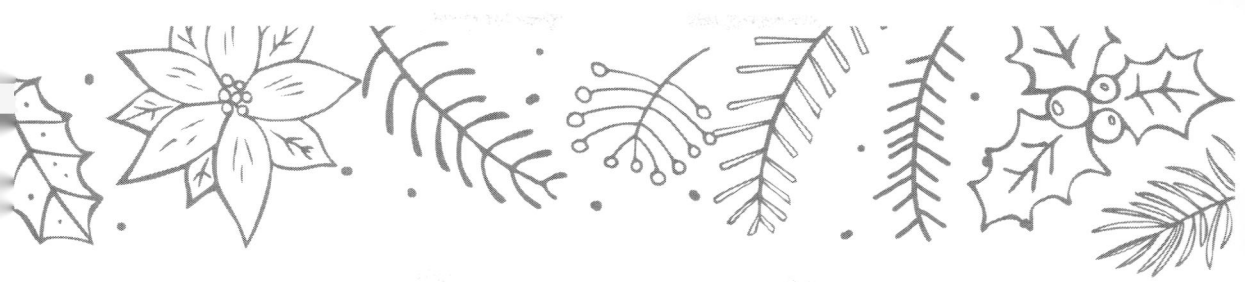

WILD
ADVENT

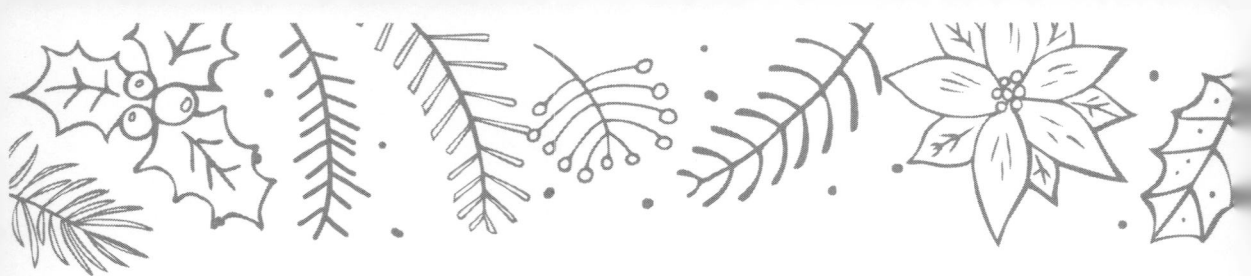

MAKE A NATIVITY SCENE

We've got a good collection of Nativity scenes in my house. Each child has their own one, which they put up each year on Advent Sunday. Each Nativity scene is different. We have one carved in olive wood from Bethlehem, one made from painted wood in Sri Lanka, and one made from playmobil. Maybe because they are so readily available, we never seem to make our own. Funny really, because you can't buy an Easter garden in the shops, and lots of people seem to make those at home.

Have a wander around an outdoor space near you, maybe your garden, or a churchyard. Maybe a park on the school run, or a woodland where you walk the dogs. What loose parts are hanging around in that space? Do any of them look like they might lend themselves to becoming a stable, or a Nativity character?

You don't have to go for formal realistic sculpture here. Representation of a Nativity set is fine. Some loose bark balanced against a rock might make a stable. You could use sticks for Mary and Joseph, and a tiny stick for baby Jesus, lying in a moss-covered manger. Dry leaves could become cloaks for wise men. Maybe some fluffy feathers could become sheep for the twig shepherds?

Waiting

You already have a good idea in your head of what a Nativity scene looks like. You know the accounts in the Bible, augmented somewhat with other random Nativity play characters. (Anyone else thinking of a donkey? Yes, me too, but no biblical accounts mention a donkey. I'll bet it was there, though.) Some people are more waiter-planners than others, who are more likely to seemingly jump straight into the doing, but everyone shares that moment when what is in their head is not yet a reality. As your eyes glance around the area you're in, your mind is matching up what you see out there with what you see in your mind's eye. Waiting, if you like, for the two to match up. This is useful waiting for us to practise. As we hold in our minds that image of Jesus, we can look at our lives, and keep watch for when the two images match up.

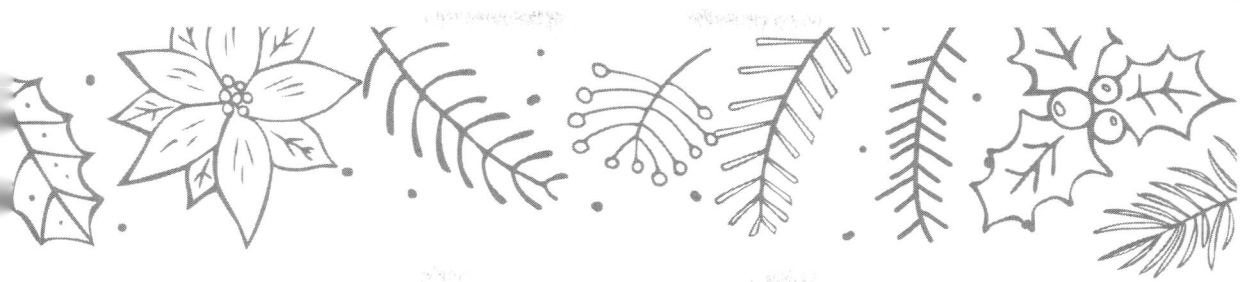

Lord, as I keep your image in my mind, the person of Jesus, help me to keep watch for when my life matches up with that image.
Amen.

Birthing

Creating a Nativity scene from scratch is a good way of meditating on the story and circumstances surrounding the birth of Jesus. It's all too easy to dress it up and whitewash it, making it all neat and tidy. Working with loose parts and found natural objects uncouples it from this, literally grounding you in the reality of God born into our real, muddy, messy Earth. A Nativity scene made of objects we rarely see through a 'religious' lens, casts new light on that familiar story, reminding us quite how shocking a story it is.

Lord, as we get our hands dirty, digging and poking at the soil, collecting and balancing sticks, stones, and other found objects, we remember you, in your glorious humanity, being born as one of us, walking on this very earth.
Amen.

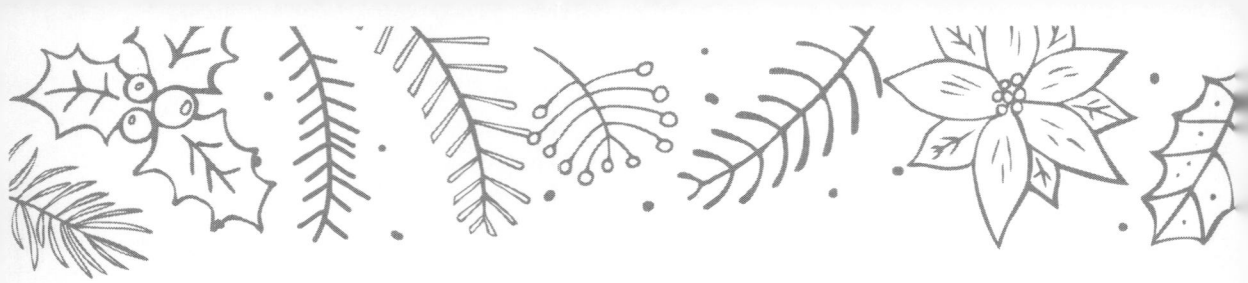

TREE ID

How well do you know your trees? You'd think that the winter was an impossible time of year to work on your tree id skills, as the trees are standing bare-branched with no clues of leaf, blossom, or fruit. However, each tree has a very distinctive pattern to its twigs. Don't forget that although it's still many months until spring, the buds are already on the trees, with their promise of the green, new life to come.

Look in the library or a bookshop for a tree id book, or search online. The Woodland Trust has good resources about trees, free of charge. You may choose to visit a local wooded area, or you could just keep an eye out for trees as you walk around your daily business. All trees are worth enjoying, even if they're just the ones planted down your street.

Try to spot twigs from the delicate birch, beech and alder, looking impossibly fragile to cope with the winter storms. The ash, oak and horse chestnut look more robust and rugged. Some species are harder to tell apart; field maple and sycamore have a similar pattern of one lead bud at the end of the twig, followed by two side buds further down. Depending on where you live, you may be able to identify the hazel from its catkins; sometimes they produce these by the end of December.

As you get better at identifying trees from their twigs, you'll find yourself spotting them all over the place, like old friends, and noticing those little budding reminders of the spring lying in wait on a regular basis.

Waiting

I found it quite striking when I realised that the new buds for the spring were already on the trees right in the depths of winter. I'd assumed that spring was when we had the hope of new growth, but no, that hope was there, lying dormant, in wait, right in the middle of the darkness and death of winter. We remember that hope lying dormant but ready to bud, the hope spoken of throughout the Old Testament, of a Messiah who would come to bring justice and righteousness, the hope lying hidden in the womb of Mary, those buds of hope waiting and ready in our lives and in the world.

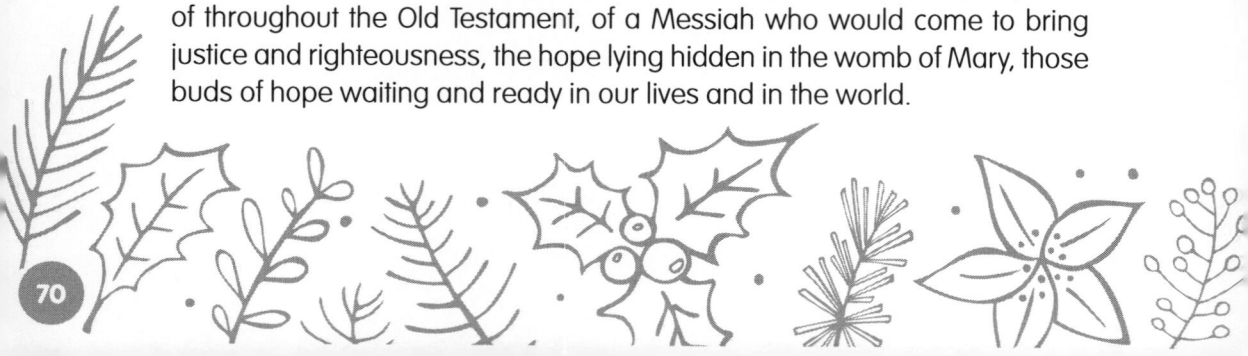

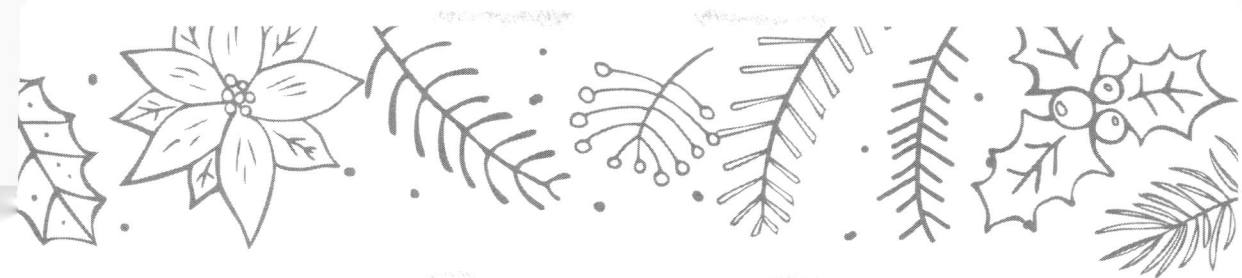

Lord, as we wait for your coming at Christmas,
show us those places where your hope lies ready to
spring up into new growth.
Amen.

Journeying

It may be that when you first began to look at the different trees, they all blended into one browny-grey twiggy mass. We begin with ignorance, but with the will to acquire knowledge. It's that will that drives us to notice the differences as well as the similarities, to check and double-check against the knowledge we have already acquired. John 16:13 tells us that the Spirit will lead us into all truth. Not truth about which twigs come from which tree, but the truth about the God who loved us into being, and sustains the whole universe. As we exercise our God-given brain, learning more and loving learning, this is good practice as we soak up more knowledge and understand more of the truth about God.

Lord, you promised that your Spirit will lead me
into all truth. As I practise enjoying learning, reveal
more truth about yourself to me.
Amen.

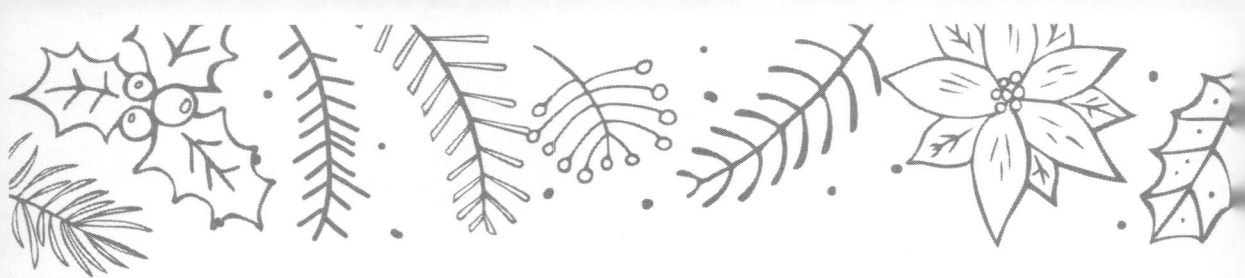

BIRD FOOD CAFÉ

The winter is a difficult time for birds and other wild creatures. The plenty of the summer and autumn is over, and yet with the colder weather, they're having to use more energy to keep themselves warm. Help them out by providing them with a smorgasbord of tasty offerings to keep their energy levels up and their hunger at bay at this cold and tricky time of year.

An easy bird feeder is an apple, cored and tied on a string. Poke sunflower seeds into the apple skin all the way round. You may find it easier to have a prodder – maybe a cocktail stick or a skewer – to make the holes with first, as sometimes the apple skin is a bit tough. Hang it up for birds to feast on.

Threading is fun, too. Collect some pipe cleaners and enjoy threading cereal hoops onto them. Threading is rhythmically therapeutic, I find! Loop your pipe cleaners round into a hoop, and hang them on the trees, like edible baubles.

Now for the messy one. Fat is an important part of the birds' diet, but you need to be careful to give them the right kind of fat. They need saturated fats for energy, which pretty much means animal fats. Lard is good to use for this, and cheap too. If you are uncomfortable using animal fat, the only other suitable fat source that I've found is coconut oil, which is high enough in saturated fats. Tip your fat into a bowl, and use your hands to squish in bird seed and maybe a little grated apple, grated cheese, or oats. I normally press blobs of this into the separate sections I've pulled off an egg carton, which I've prepared by threading a string through a small hole in the bottom, then threading a stick through from side to side to enable the birds to perch while they feast.

Accepting

Feeding the birds makes you feel warm inside and good about yourself. You imagine their gratitude as they discover the food you've prepared for them. And that's not wrong – it's nice to think of others and their needs. However, I don't know about you, but I know I sometimes find it much harder to accept help, to accept what others are offering me. I find it much easier to be a

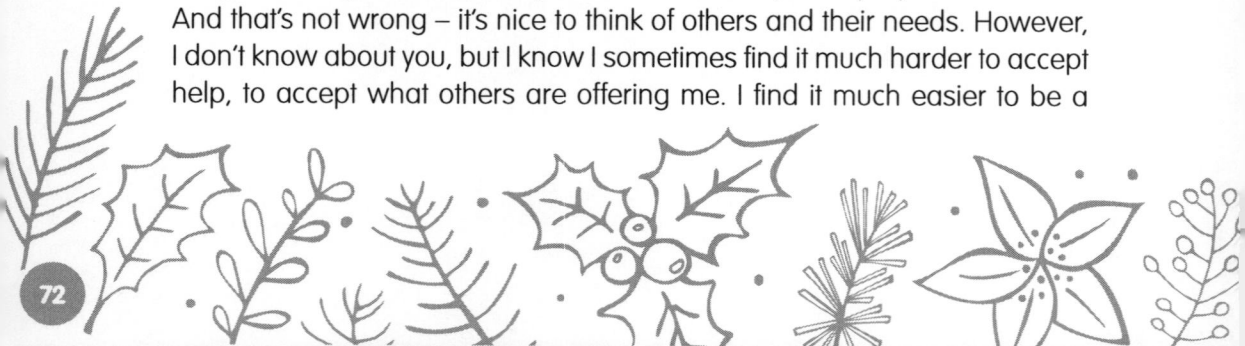

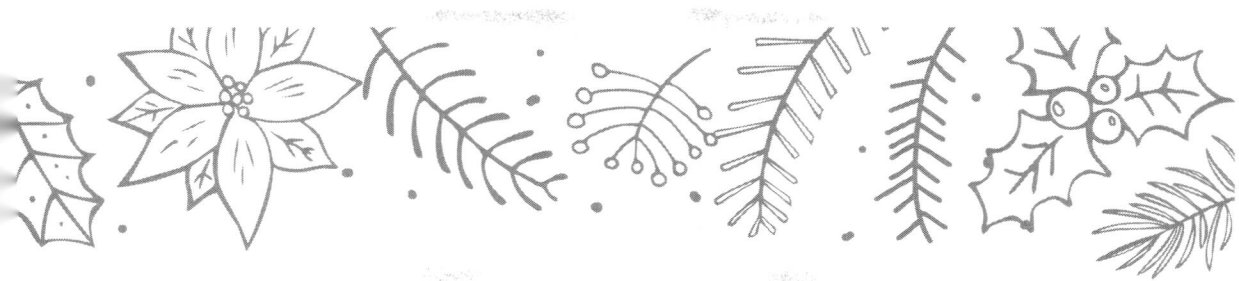

bird feeder than a hungry bird. To accept help, to accept a gift, makes us vulnerable, and we can find that uncomfortable. However, this gift of God-with-us is offered to us, no strings attached. We need to practise accepting graciously. Watch the birds, pecking at the food you've left out for them, and learn from them. They're good at that.

> Lord, give me the humility and the courage to
> accept the gifts you give me.
> Amen.

Birthing

What is it that feeds you? I don't mean jacket potatoes and biscuits, your equivalent of lard and seed cakes, but what is it that feeds and sustains you through the dark and cold seasons of your life? As you squish, and thread, and poke, preparing the food for the birds, reflect on who and what feeds and sustains you, and give thanks. Make a mental note to seek these people and things out, to see them, contact them, or do them more often. Remember the words of Jesus in Matthew 6:26-34. As the birds are fed, so also will God provide for you. And sometimes it will be through the actions of other people.

> Lord, as I feed the birds, help me to trust that you
> will keep me fed with everything I need.
> Amen.

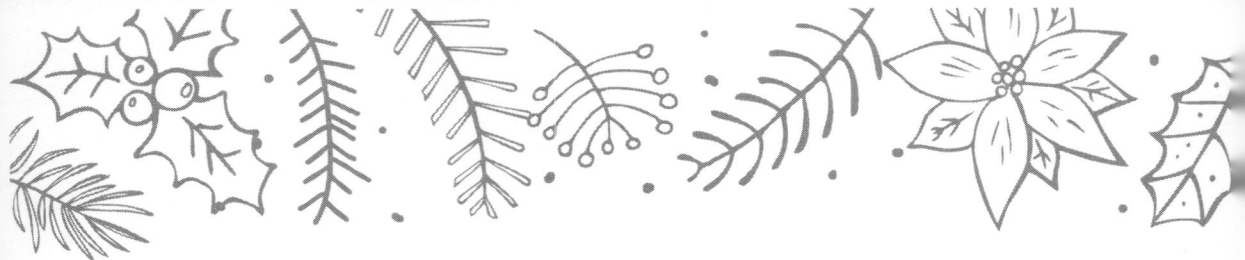

MAKE A WREATH

It's easy to pick up a wreath to decorate your home at this time of year. They're sold in cheap high street shops, and in posh florists. Around here you can even pay a lot of money to be taught to make your own in a class where you'll be provided with willow, greenery, secateurs and wire. Their origin lies in the traditions of yule, the idea of greenery in the winter showing hope in a time of death and decay, of the promise of new life to come.

Why not have a go yourself? Take your secateurs off for a walk outside. Find yourself some bendy wood – willow is great – and cut a few good long lengths of this. Cut lengths of ivy, maybe some laurel, some holly with berries if you can find it, maybe some mistletoe. Grasp a bundle of your bendy sticks and twist them together. Keep going, shaping it into a circle, adding a new stick every now and again. When you meet the place you began, tuck and weave the ends into the twisted strands of wood. This should hold the bendy sticks firmly in a circular wreath shape.

Next, weave the greenery and berries in and around your basic wreath. Often florists will work with odd numbers, so give that a go and see if it looks better. You can use short pieces of florists' wire to attach your greenery if it needs a little help. Quite often you can still find crab apples on the ground at this time of year – wiring these into your wreath will add a nice splash of colour, and a tasty snack for any birds visiting your front door.

Accepting

When you're coaxing a wreath into shape, you need to take your time. If you force it, the bendy sticks will snap. If you tuck them in too brutally, they'll break. Hold the sticks, feel which way they want to bend. Try to use their natural inclination to get them to almost weave themselves. Use the contrast in their springiness to add strength to the weave rather than force it apart. When you're working with others, remember what your sticks have taught you as you weaved them. Use what everyone can offer, so you can all work together more effectively. God does this, too. He is able to weigh up and

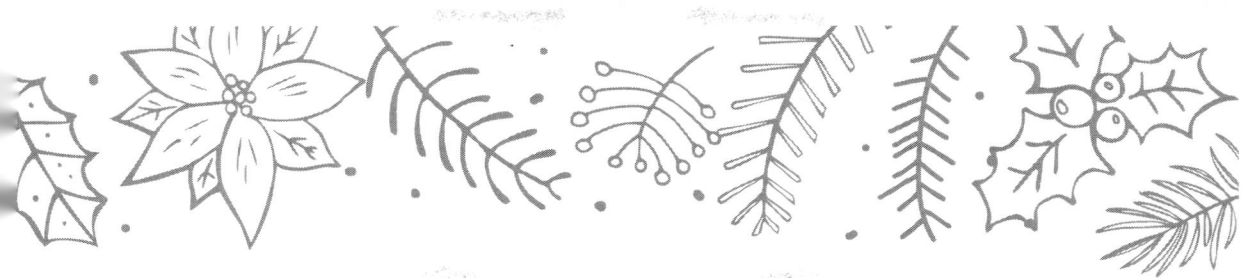

judge your natural inclination, and use it so the shape you end up in fits you perfectly. God never pushes you to be the person you are not.

> Lord, you use me and accept me just the way I am.
> Thank you.
> Amen.

Journeying

The action of weaving in and out and through your wreath can act a little like a meditation, like walking around a labyrinth. As the material you are weaving moves, it travels around, back past where it started. It revisits points along the way, but from a different perspective. It sometimes runs alongside a length of ivy, or cosies up to red holly berries, before diverting off on another route. As you weave, reflect on your life's journey, of the path that it has taken, of the places and people you've come up against on the way, of those you've drifted away from. Of how the way your life is woven in with others, and this is what makes it strong. Think of God the weaver, coaxing you and tucking you into the right paths for you.

> Lord, thank you for guiding me on my journey through life. Show me where I resist your guiding hand, weaving me into the places I need to go, and give me the courage to be pliable, ready to listen as you shape me.
> Amen.

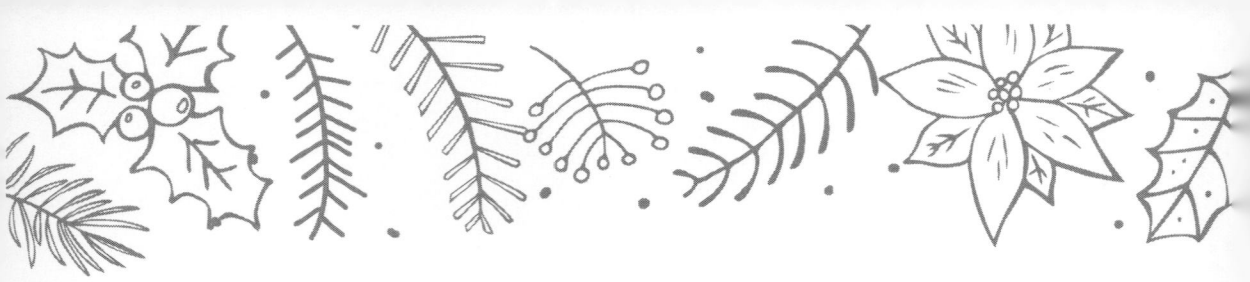

NOTES

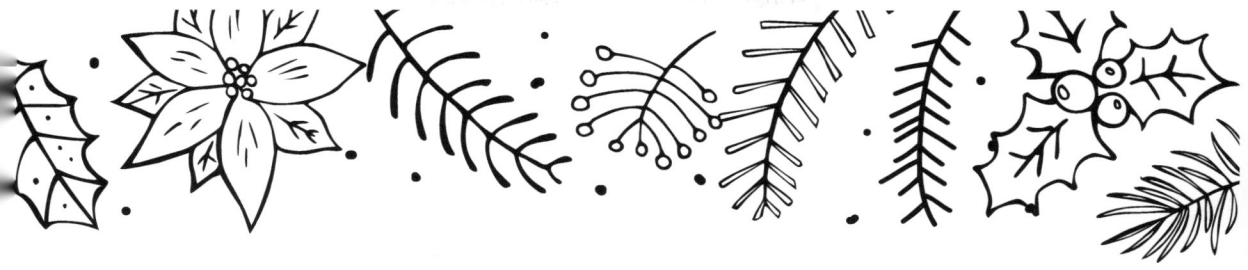

EVEN SHORTER THINGS TO DO

Even shorter things to do...

Watch the sky change colour at sunset

See
page
84

Find some holly and ivy -
and sing the song!

See
page
86

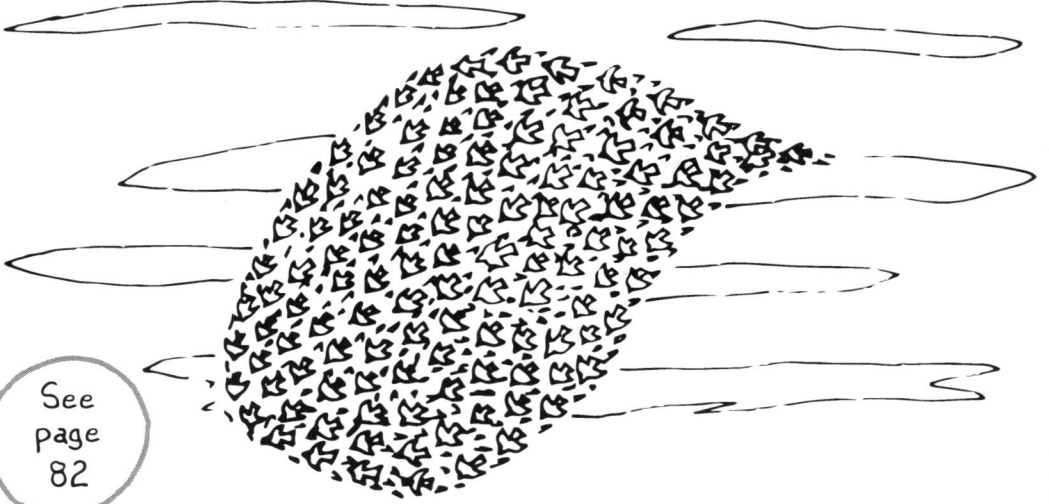

See page 82

Watch a murmuration of starlings

Turn your heating down
by 1°C - and put on
a jumper

See page 88

See page 80

listen to the birds
go to bed

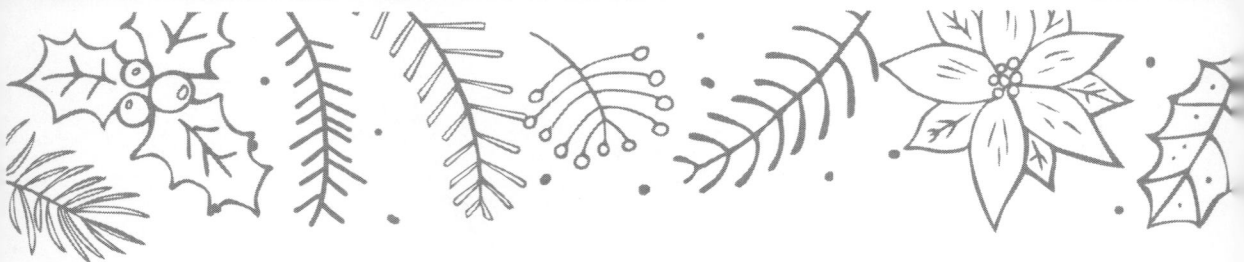

LISTEN TO THE BIRDS GO TO BED

Every year we make a date to go out and listen to the dawn chorus in the spring. But with the early onset of dark evenings in the winter, the birds make quite a racket as they head off to bed. The advantage of this is that you don't have to wake up early to head out to listen to them, either!

The songs they sing will be different to a spring dawn chorus. Some of the birds who join in with that don't spend the winter in the UK, and some of those birds save their singing for the spring. But there are plenty of birds who will make a noise, and although some of them are more noise than music, there's a harsh and strident quality to it that suits the winter landscape.

Sparrows will chirp all year round, and the sound of crows cawing in the bare, winter trees is very evocative of this time of year. The chatter of starlings, collecting in flocks at dusk, is varied with rattles and trills, whistles and warbles. They are excellent mimics and in an urban environment will copy not just other birds but other sounds they hear through the day. Where I live, there are flocks of ring-necked parakeets, which make an almighty squawking fuss as they come in to roost for the night. Robins are one of the only songbirds that sing through the winter. Their autumn song is less upbeat than their spring song, but it's sometimes over the middle of December that their song changes from one to the other, getting stronger and more powerful.

Waiting

We often talk of waiting on God – the act of attentive waiting being one of prayer. Attentive listening is good practice for this. To listen well, you need to still yourself; not just your body and your voice, but also your mind. Absorb and soak in the atmosphere around yourself. As your mind empties of plans for dinner and worries about work, you're able to notice the sound of the birds. At first, as just a noise, and then you can pick out different voices, calling from different places. The harshness of the crow's call, the purity of the robin's song, the noisy chaos of the parakeets. When you pray, remember

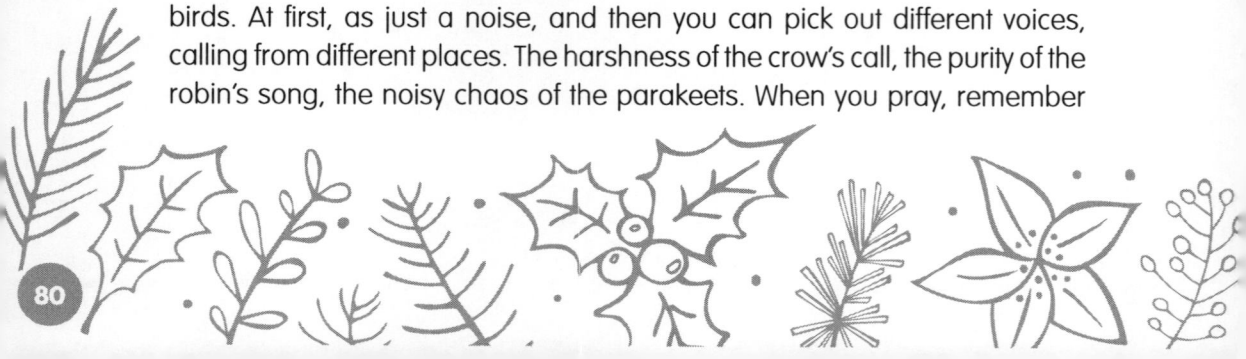

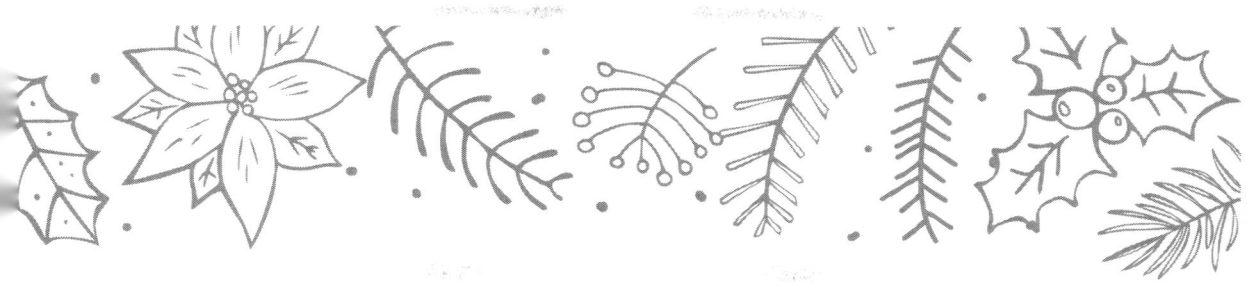

how you stilled yourself, and were able to tune in to hear what was there all along. It's similar with listening to God.

> Lord, as I still myself to listen to the birds, help me
> still myself to listen to you.
> Amen.

Accepting

It takes a little mental effort to recalibrate your expectations when listening to winter birdsong. You won't get that lyrical experience of the spring, and it can be tempting to dismiss it as worthless noise. But it is beautiful in its own way, and spending your time wishing for it to be something different will mean you miss out on enjoying its own uniqueness. What is unique about who you are, about your gifts, about your life? Teach yourself to accept the gifts that God has given you, and to use them for his glory.

> Lord, thank you for giving me my own unique gifts,
> and give me the courage to own them.
> Amen.

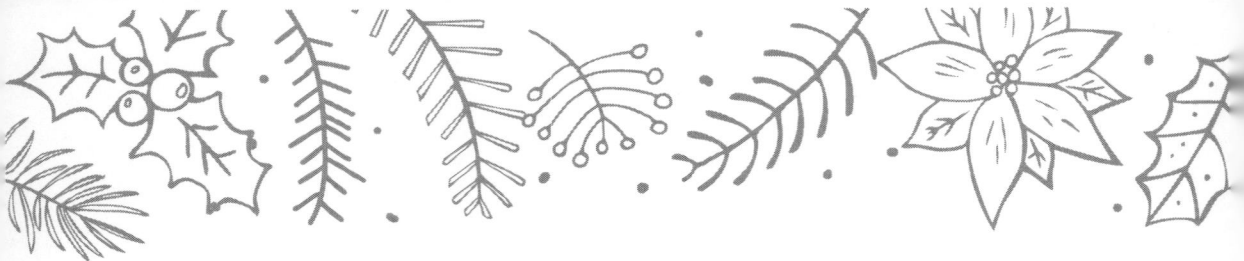

WATCH A MURMURATION

The flocks of starlings over the winter create one of the most impressive spectacles of nature seen in the UK. From being a noisy, chaotic, chattering muddle, when it's dusk, they gather in great numbers to roost. Moving as one, they take to the air, forming a pattern that swirls and shifts in the sky before suddenly all dropping back down to the land.

Starlings do always live in flocks, but it's over the winter, when their numbers are boosted by starlings overwintering in the UK, that they reach these breathtakingly massive sizes. It's believed that starlings live in a flock because there's safety in numbers, and the more starlings there are, the less chance each one has of being taken by an airborne predator. It's also possible that the heat from thousands of starlings roosting together can make the roost a tiny fraction warmer, which could save lives in extremely cold weather. Tracking starling movements shows that each starling moves around within the flock, trying to give itself the least time on the vulnerable edge as possible. Starlings have split-second reactions, so when one starling chooses to change direction, the whole flock can move almost instantly, giving this mesmerising display in the air.

The best place for you to try to spot a local starling murmuration is near a reed bed, a pier, or failing that, somewhere with trees, hedges, or buildings where you've seen starlings roosting. If the day has been bright, they may come in to roost later; if the day has been overcast, they may come in to roost earlier than sunset. Some nights they will come in to roost small group by small group, maybe flying in low, so there will be nothing amazing to see. Murmurations don't seem to be affected by weather. Nobody is quite sure why some nights the birds put on a display and some nights they don't. So, you may get lucky, or you may not. I'll cross my fingers that it's the former for you!

Journeying

The starlings flying in a group move through the air seemingly as one. They turn on a wingtip, swirling through the sky. They take turns to fly on the outer edge of the flock, the place where it's more dangerous. As a Christian

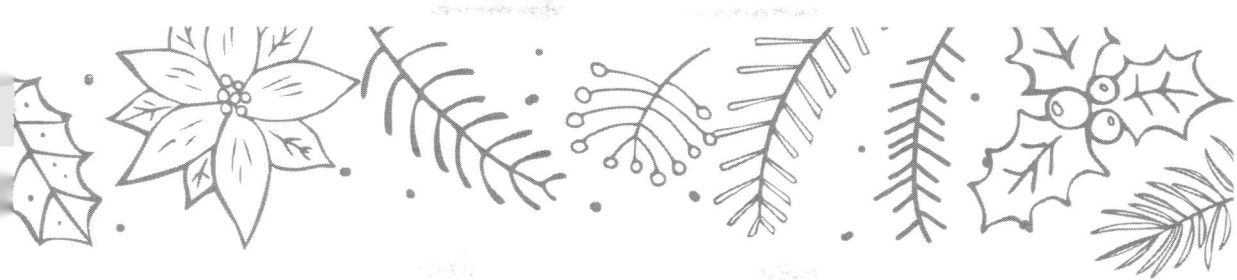

community, how are we like this flock of starlings? How does this flock of starlings inspire us in our community life? We are called to be one body, relying on each other and caring for each other. Remind yourself of the words in 1 Corinthians 12:12-27 as you watch the starling flock.

Lord, as the starlings flock together in flight and in rest, show me how to play a full part in my own community, and to be cared for in turn.
Amen.

Birthing

Often we think of new things being brought to birth as coming from great periods of planning, painful organisational feats, and long waiting. Here are the starlings showing us a different way. They don't sit down in groups throughout the summer, with a flipchart and markers, looking through endless powerpoint presentations, splitting up into focus groups, to work out the perfect flight pattern for their display. They move instinctively, guided by one another, and make it look effortless. Maybe we should sometimes listen to and be inspired by those who plan on the hoof, who are flexible creators, who may drive us crazy with their lack of a plan or attention to detail, but can free us up to explore new avenues we'd never have gone down otherwise. In Galations 5:25 (NIV) we read the words, 'Since we live by the Spirit, let us keep in step with the Spirit' – we need to follow the Spirit, wingtip to wingtip.

Lord, as I watch the starlings swirl, moving as one, I pray that your Church may be one.
Amen.

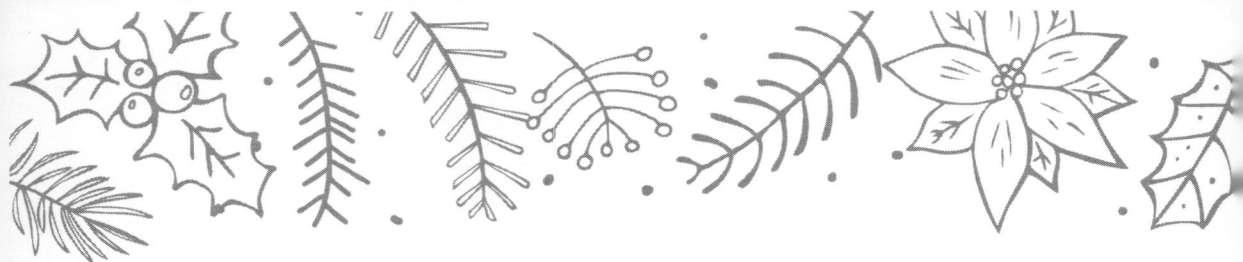

WATCH THE SKY CHANGE COLOUR

A spectacular sunset is one of those classic summer holiday shots to share on facebook or Instagram, proclaiming to the world how these amazing colours are #nofilter. The reds, oranges, yellows, and purples of a lovely sunset make me catch my breath each time I see one, and although the sunset soon fades, its beauty doesn't fade from my memory. Sunsets don't just belong to summer holidays, though. You're as likely to see one in the winter as in the summer.

As the angle between the sun and where you are decreases, and the sun appears to drop in the sky, the light is passing through a greater distance of the earth's atmosphere. The shorter wavelengths of light, those on the green and blue end of the spectrum, are scattered before they can reach you, leaving the longer wavelength orange and red colours lighting up the sky that you see. Because the atmosphere bends light, by the time you see the sun actually setting, it has already dropped below the horizon – it's just that its rays of light are being refracted so they still hit your vision. It's like you can see right round the curvature of the earth for just a moment.

For a truly great sunset, there needs to be some cloud formation in the sky. Not low-level clouds, which would prevent the light from the sun from reaching you sufficiently, but mid or high-level clouds. These will reflect the colour spectrum reaching them, in the same way that they reflect white light in the daytime. Feel free to snap the sunset and share it, but don't forget to stand and stare at it, soaking it in, too.

Waiting

In Advent we are waiting for the coming of Jesus, born as a baby thousands of years ago in Bethlehem. We are waiting, and yet we already know the story. We are waiting, and yet we already know something of the implications of this universe-shattering event. What on earth is the value in waiting for something that has already occurred? As we wait for the sun to dip below the horizon, it appears to hang there for a moment. The astrological sunset, where the sun has moved below our horizon, has already happened, and

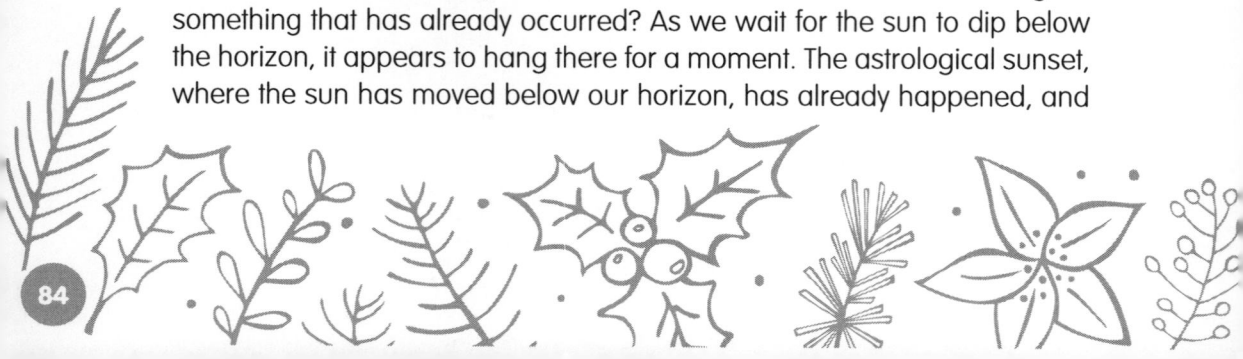

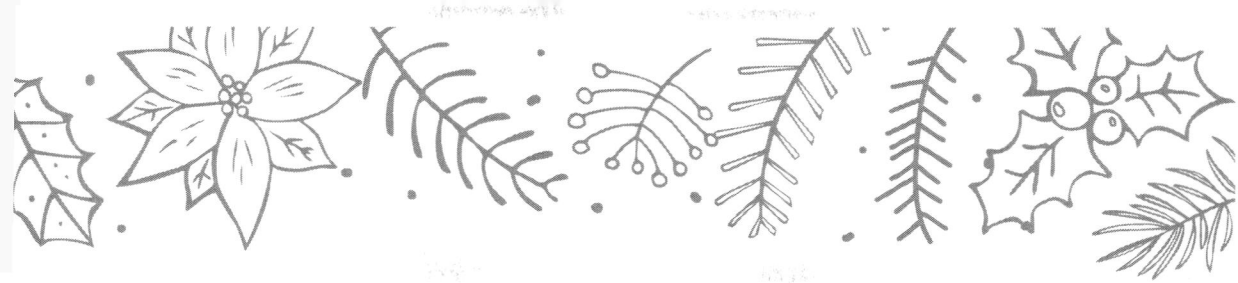

yet we are still standing, gazing at the sun. Sometimes we are still waiting, when an event has occurred. We're waiting because we know that the full impact is still working its way out. We are still waiting for this Jesus, born so long ago, to be born again in our lives, changing them and redeeming them.

> Lord, in this time of Advent, caught between the 'now' and the 'not yet', shine the light of your presence on us.
> Amen.

Journeying

In the daytime, we barely notice the light. We take it as obvious, our entitlement for the period between the morning and the evening. It's when the light has a more complicated journey that we see it bursting into colour in the sky. As the light waves travel through a longer and longer stretch of our earth's atmosphere, we are more aware of their beauty, and the colours that have actually been there all along, invisibly mixed into white light. As we travel through our life's journey, do our true colours start to shine out? How has our life's journey brought out our innate beauty?

> Lord, as you lead me through my life's journey, help my true colours to shine.
> Amen.

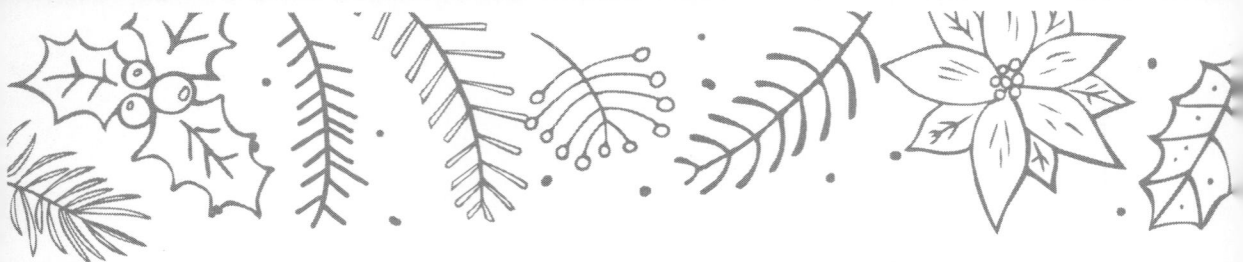

THE HOLLY AND THE IVY

'The holly and the ivy when they are both full grown, of all the trees that are in the wood, the holly bears the crown.'

I guarantee you won't have to travel far to find a holly bush or some straggling ivy. Holly is a hardy tree, fighting for a chance for life in all manner of waste spaces, as well as planted for a green and red display of seasonal colour at this time of year. Ivy is even more widespread. Find any patch of wall that's not been tidied to within an inch of its life, and you're more than likely to find some ivy clinging on and climbing up it.

Holly, as the song goes, bears a berry as red as any blood. In fact, only the female holly plants bear berries – but you'll need both in reasonably close proximity to guarantee winter colour. Although the holly berry is toxic for humans, it's an important food source for some birds in the winter, which probably explains how the tiny holly plants seem to spring up all over the place – the seeds they have germinated from have travelled away from the parent plant inside a bird's stomach!

In the traditional mythology of these islands, the year was divided up between two woodland kings – King Oak, and King Holly. King Holly rules the year between midsummer and midwinter, so around Advent time King Holly is in his final few days. You'd assume, wouldn't you, that it's Holly taking precedence around Christmas, but actually it's King Oak, bursting through triumphantly with his promise of new life to come in the darkness of winter, that gets the upper hand at the solstice. Spot any parallels with the Christian story there?

Ivy is a clinging plant – look carefully and you'll see the tiny suckers where it attaches itself to the host trunk, or to your wall or garden fence. It's pretty resilient; you may have a gardening blitz where you tear it all down, and pull it all off, but seemingly before you know it, it's climbing up again. In the grey-brown gloom of winter, it is constantly, tenaciously green.

As you spend some time with your holly and your ivy, maybe you'd like to sing the words through of that Christmas carol, and see how they illustrate these tenets of your faith.

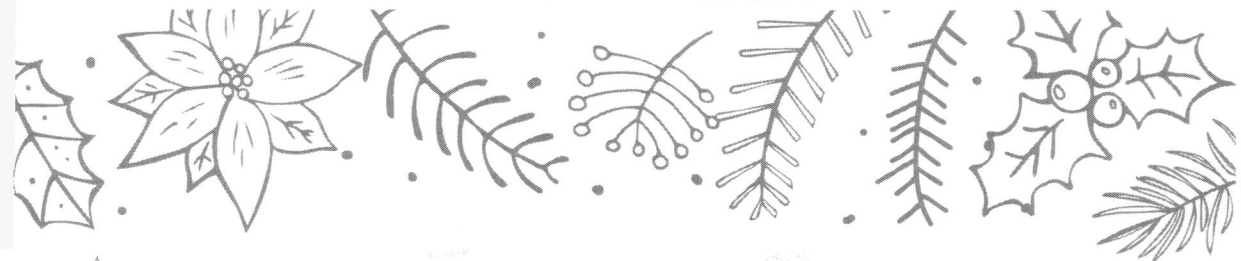

Accepting

There are lots of berries that I like. Raspberries, blackberries, blueberries, strawberries are all delicious. I try to grow some of them in my garden in the summer, with mixed success. We have more luck picking blackberries from hedgerows in the autumn, to freeze and stir into our morning porridge. Holly berries though – I can't eat those. They're no good for me, so does that mean they're useless? Obviously not – just because they're not edible for humans doesn't mean that they're not useful and tasty for other creatures who share my neighbourhood. Just as different species have different needs and different tastes, so also do all of us, in what we find helpful, or uplifting. In the things that we find bring us closer to God. It's easy to feel that our way is 'right', but no matter how satisfying we may find a bowl of cherries, and how badly we would react to a bowl of holly berries, that's not universally true. What is true is that we all need to eat. Try to have a conversation with someone who worships in a very different way to you. Listen to what they find valuable and what they cherish, and remember that it's the need to worship which is the thing you both have in common.

> Lord, you made us all different. Help me to accept
> and rejoice in our difference.
> Amen.

Birthing

Both these plants speak to us strongly of resilient life in difficult places. They are both evergreens, keeping their leaves through the winter. Both these plants play a pivotal role in providing shelter and food for a wide range of creatures. It's thought that over thirty different species of invertebrates directly rely on holly, and ivy supports a whole variety of rare creatures with its flowers, its fat-filled berries, and its tangling protection. As God provides for us in difficult places, this helps us to grow so that we, in turn, can provide protection and feed others.

> Lord, as you have cared for me, so help me care
> for others.
> Amen.

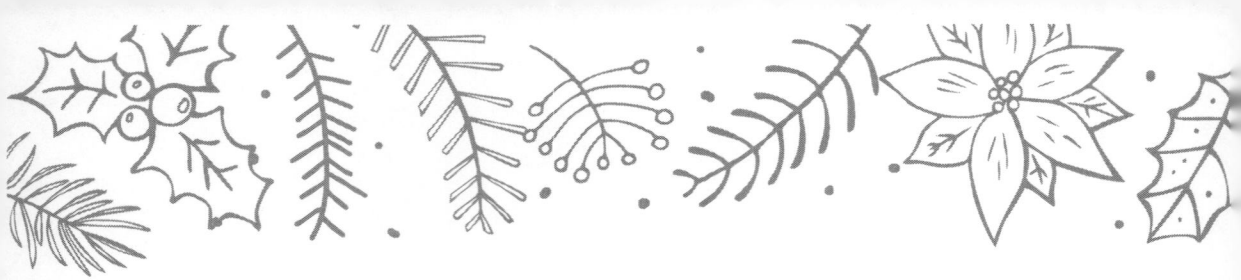

TURN THE THERMOSTAT DOWN

This is an activity that takes place indoors. It may seem strange that I'm including it as an activity in a Wild Advent book, where the emphasis is on finding God, and listening to God outdoors. But this is an activity that will have repercussions outside the confines of your home.

Simply turn your thermostat down. Just one degree. If you normally keep your home at a toasty 25 degrees, see if you can cope at 24. If you normally keep things ticking along at 18, would you be that much colder at 17? How low can you go?

Obviously, I don't want you all shivering in your shirt sleeves and cursing me. But take a moment to think more creatively about what heating you actually need. Is heating all the air in your home the best way to stay warm? Have a go at heating yourself. Get something warm inside you, like a cup of tea, coffee, or hot chocolate, so you carry your own personal hot water bottle in your stomach. Make sure you're wearing enough layers – put on a jumper, or a cardie or poncho on top if you're wearing one already. I have one of those circular scarves that goes on in October and doesn't come off until March! If you work from home, or spend a lot of time there, make sure you get up and move around every so often (your back will thank you, too) – or consider working from the local library or a coffee shop, and taking advantage of their heating system that's on already.

So why is this Wild? Well, not only will this save you money, but using less energy will reduce your carbon emissions by up to 360kg. Yes, there are bigger carbon-wasting baddies out there, and you may feel that you reducing your emissions is a mere drop in the ocean, but don't forget, the ocean is made up of millions of drops.

Waiting

The problems with global warming, with pollution, with over-consumption in our planet feel overwhelming. I've yet to meet someone who wasn't affected by the *Blue Planet* series and its message about plastic in our oceans. From being the preserve of a few people perceived as a bit odd, environmentalism

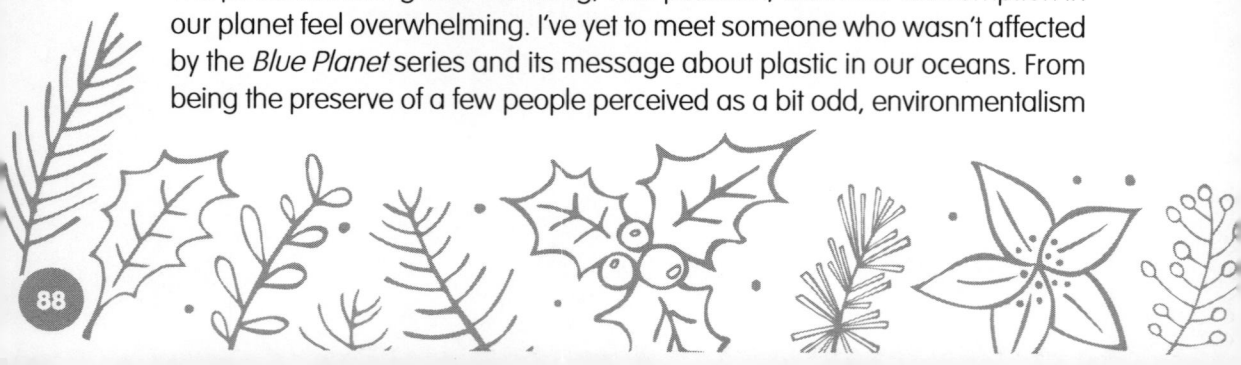

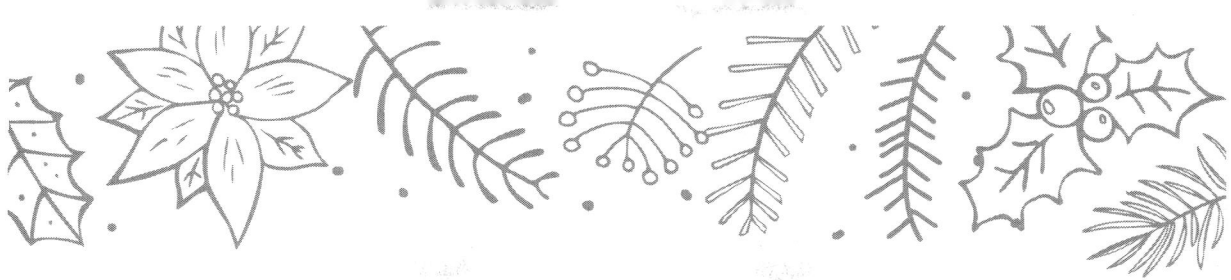

is nudging its way into the familiar and normal. When there's a task so huge, the temptation is to wait for someone to do something. For someone to come up with a solution. We can feel as if our impact will be so small that there's no point us even trying. When we feel this, remember Jesus' words from Matthew 13:33. We are called to be like that tiny quantity of yeast, working its way through to leaven the whole loaf. As Christians, if we stir up environmental change, looking after the creation we've been given, who knows what huge things could happen?

> Lord, as my heart aches for what has been done to your good creation, agitate me to make small changes, so that these small changes can, through your power, become something great.
> Amen.

Journeying

We all have to start somewhere. Often making a decision to begin, to try out something new, to change something that needs changing, results in us beginning a journey that leads us to places we never imagined we'd go. One thing leads to another. As you turn down your heating, you start to notice what's going in your rubbish bin. As you start to recycle more, you wonder how you can dispose of your food waste more ethically. As you start to cut down on your takeaway coffee cups, you notice the rest of the single-use plastic you dispose of every day. Similarly, as we practise patience, we notice our selfishness. As we try to control our anger, we notice also our greed. Jesus takes us by the hand, and leads us step by step.

> Lord, show me your path and I will follow you.
> Amen.

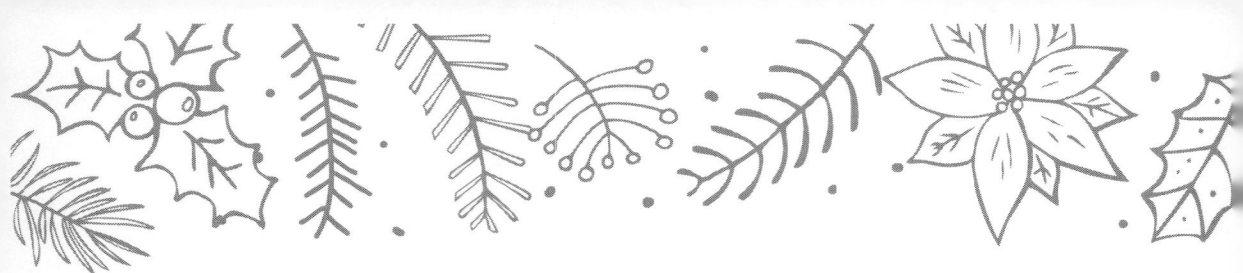

THEMATIC INDEX

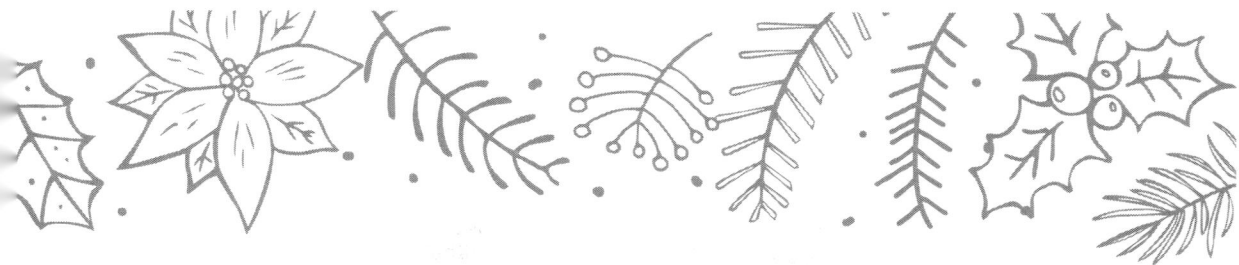

IN PRAISE OF WILD ADVENT

The approach to Christmas may not be the most obvious time to spend outdoors, but with all the research linking human well-being to time spent in the natural world, perhaps it is more important than ever at the time of year we are inclined to huddle up indoors or stress about the Christmas to-do list. Rachel's book beautifully opens our eyes to the wonder of the ordinary and reminds us to go with the flow and find something to enjoy, even on days when the weather isn't to our choosing! Through suggestions of simple activities, using all our senses, she encourages us to take time to notice the ordinary miracles all around us. Short prayers remind us that these ordinary miracles have their source in God, whose creativity continues to astound us. Christmas will be all the more joyful for an Advent spent outdoors.

Revd Cate Williams, Mission and Evangelism Officer, Gloucester Diocese

Rachel Summers has once again invited us to notice the world in which we live and to see God in every part of it. With skill, humour and depth, she encourages us to notice the world around us, to connect with it in simple, yet meaningful, ways. This noticing and connecting lead us to a groundedness in God and Creation which brings us home. At a time of year when family time is often short-changed, Rachel highlights its importance and offers a richness for the whole season. This book is a blessing.

Revd Dr Bob Root, The United Church of Canada

Even though I know from previous experience that being outdoors makes me (and my children) feel happier and calmer, it's so very easy to forget this in winter. It's all the more easy to forget in the weeks leading up to Christmas which can feel overwhelmingly busy. This book helps to put 'time in nature' at the top of that December to-do list in a playful and practical way. I found the reflections at the end of each section really accessible and thought-provoking. They deepened

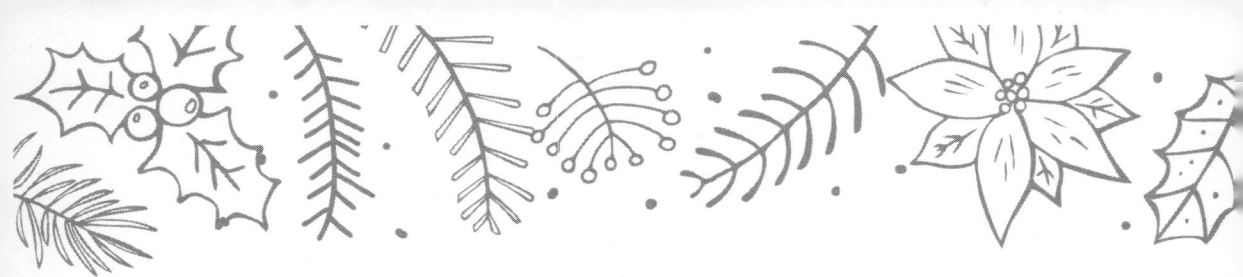

IN PRAISE OF WILD ADVENT
CONTINUED

my understanding and appreciation of the suggested activities, helping me to approach them with openness and curiosity. Rachel's wonderful book will help you and your family to find joy and meaning in the season of waiting.

Nessa Tierney, Mum of two boys

Christians often speak about saying prayers, as if prayer were something that only happens in your head and spills out of your mouth. But Rachel Summers' lovely *Wild Advent* book paints another picture, reasserting an ancient truth that prayer is also something you do. It happens in your fingers and your feet. It is dancing as well as speaking. Making as well as thinking. Waiting as well as declaring. It is an expression of joy, wonder, delight and longing. And as this is an Advent book, that time when the church gets ready to greet a word made flesh, then this little book is about making Advent real with all your energy and creativity and with the whole of your being.

The Rt Revd Stephen Cottrell, Bishop of Chelmsford

Brilliant book. I've just finished reading it and I want to go into my back garden and lie on the ground and imagine gravity stopping me falling into the depths of the stars. This book will inspire anyone who wants to explore Advent and learn to love nature, people and God a little bit more. Practical, simple, reflective, warm and fun activities that everyone can join in for 5 minutes or whole days (or nights) out. Great stuff, Rachel!

Andrew Dye, Forest School Practitioner

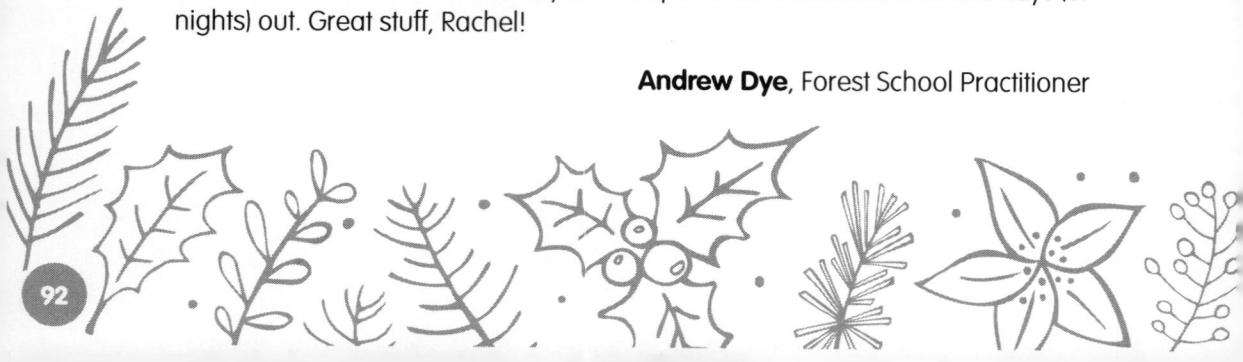